Cross Connections

Cross Connections

A Life's Story about One Pastor's Ministry of
Connecting the Episodes of Family, Church,
Friends, Mentors, and Events

James G. Cobb

RESOURCE *Publications* · Eugene, Oregon

CROSS CONNECTIONS
A Life's Story about One Pastor's Ministry of Connecting the Episodes of
Family, Church, Friends, Mentors, and Events

Resource Publications
An Imprint of Wipf and Stock Publishers
199 W. 8th Ave., Suite 3
Eugene, OR 97401

www.wipfandstock.com

PAPERBACK ISBN: 978-1-6667-3580-2
HARDCOVER ISBN: 978-1-6667-9326-0
EBOOK ISBN: 978-1-6667-9327-7

01/13/22

To my wife, the Rev. Judith A. Cobb, for her love
and devotion to husband, children and Church. Her
joy is contagious, her intuition is Spirit-infiltrated,
her instincts about people, uncanny! She has been a
partner in ministry and every church served by her has
received creativity, energy and inspiration and a boost in
motivation to follow Christ and serve to God's glory!

·

Contents

Acknowledgments | ix
Preface | xi

1   Even the First Year was Eventful | 1
2   The Early Years and the Case for Original Sin | 3
3   Thankful for Faith Formation | 7
4   Urban and Rural: A Contrasted Life | 11
5   Beginning of Life Discernment of Right and Wrong | 14
6   The Indelible Imprinting of Senior High (1963–65) | 20
7   Academic Imprinting for Life | 25
8   Theology Formation and Some Surprises | 30
9   An Aside about Ruth and Eric Gritsch | 39
10   Thoughts about Parish Ministry | 41
11   St. Martin Lutheran Church, Annapolis, MD (1973–74) | 46
12   Christ Lutheran Church, Fredericksburg, VA (1974–81) | 51
13   Trinity Lutheran Church, Grand Rapids, MI (1981–88) | 60
14   First Lutheran Church, Norfolk, VA (1988–99) | 72
15   Associate Dean, Lutheran Theological Seminary, Gettysburg, PA (1999–2006) | 91
16   Ascension Lutheran Church, Towson, MD (2006–14) | 96
17   Retirement: What's That? | 104

Appendix 1: Laughing through the Church with a Three-Year Old | 109
Bibliography | 135

Acknowledgments

I WISH TO THANK my editor who read and helped correct my manuscript with many helpful suggestions: Ms. Jennifer Bateman, a fine editor who also happens to be my niece! Many thanks!

Preface

EVEN AS I STARTED this project and before I wrote a word, Judy asked, "Why are you writing?" I answered, "First, I want to tell some of my life's story (autobiography) but I see it interwoven with accepting the Church as a "funny place." Every pastor has comic stories about church foibles, some involving weddings and even funerals, but the humor is known only by God because so few clergy write about their memories. The Church knows much humor and we, of all people, can laugh at ourselves.

Secondly, I am truly humbled to see how God has made some unbelievable "connections" across formation, with the people and events that must point us to deep gratitude for the God who has the whole world in his hands.

Thirdly, my favorite writer, Frederick Buechner, says, "Listen to your life. Listen to what happens to you. For it is in what happens to you that God speaks. It is a language not easy to decipher. God is there powerfully, memorably, unforgettably."[1] Also, Buechner adds, "Listen to your life. All moments are key moments. I discovered that if you really keep your eyes peeled to it and your ears open, if you really pay attention to it, even such a limited and limiting life as the one I was living . . . opened up onto extraordinary vistas. Taking your children to school, kissing your wife goodbye. Eating lunch with a friend. Trying to do a decent

---

1. Buechner, *Listening to Your Life*, 2.

day's work. Hearing the rain patter against the window. There is no event so commonplace but that God is present within it, always hiddenly, always leaving you room to recognize him or not to recognize him, but all the more fascinatingly because of that, all the more compellingly and hauntingly."[2] If I were called upon to state in a few words the essence of everything I was trying to say both as a novelist and as a preacher, it would be something like this: Listen to your life. See it for the fathomless mystery that it is. In the boredom and pain of it no less than in the excitement and gladness: touch, taste, smell your way to the holy and hidden hear of it because in the last analysis all moments are key moments, and life itself is grace."[3]

Lastly, I cannot believe how "looking back" can be so instructive of how people and events cluster to truly be a "formation" of one's vocation. These pages may also reveal that a look back to see how the Gospel of Jesus Christ has been a source of my "subtle resistance" to the ways of the world. The Gospel has helped me to consider a different world view with regard to poverty, race, gender, LGBTQAI issues and the stance we must sometimes take against the culture and mores of a fallen world. Then, there is the matter of standing back and seeing a big picture and being awestruck by connecting the dots of family, church friends, mentors and events. Stay tuned . . .

I hope you will enjoy these pages . . .

JGC
Aug. 2021

---

2. Buechner, *Now and Then*, 92.

3. Buechner, *Now and Then*, 87.

CHAPTER 1

Even the First Year was Eventful

MY PARENTS AND GRANDPARENTS were driving on a two-lane highway when my grandfather approached a curving uphill road near North Wilkesboro, NC and apparently, blinded by the sun, he went over the road's edge and overturned the vehicle down an embankment. All four adults were seriously injured and all were hospitalized for at least 6 weeks. They sustained fractured skulls, broken legs, and hips. Apparently, I was thrown out of an open car window (days before infant car seats or seat belts), and was caught in a bush with minor scratches. A mountaineer couple heard the crash, found me and called an ambulance. I am told that I was taken to aunts and then grandparents for at least a couple of months. When my Mom regained consciousness in the hospital, she was sure I had not survived and could not be consoled. As Dad recovered from injuries, she would come home to lie in a prone position for some time. I could be lifted to her but probably was left to later crawl the room and explore. I think the "bush" was not exactly a Moses story but seemed like its own miracle. In a few years, I remember my Dad's permission to pull books from his shelves, make highways and roll cars and trucks over the books, self—entertaining for hours. My parents' return to health after 8–12 weeks seemed complete and no other complications from the accident seemed apparent.

CHAPTER 2

The Early Years and the Case for Original Sin

I COME FROM A long line of Lutheran pastors. I am a third-generation pastor and happen to have had three uncles and a couple of cousins and a nephew in this ministry. Things didn't start out that way. In early parsonage life, I helped out with the family's preparation for Sunday worship. When old enough, the Saturday regimen included shoe polishing, bulletin folding (Immanuel Lutheran, Blountville, TN and Emmanuel Lutheran, Roanoke, VA) and in one new mission congregation, setting up folding chairs and a card table for an altar in a lodge hall (Messiah Lutheran, Knoxville, TN). In some of my early memories, I remember having some of my fun curtailed. With three of us kids under age five, my mother sat as a single parent most Sundays and had her hands full! One Sunday, I lay on the church floor under a pew. When she pulled me out by my ankles, after the sermon, I had found wads of chewing gum stuck under the pews (by others' delinquent behaviors) and had enjoyed a blissful time of ten-fingered string art for entertainment! Another Sunday, I sneaked comic books stuffed in my shirt for the service. When she confiscated the forbidden books (1950's), she sat on them for the whole service (our worship included standing, kneeling, etc.). Others asked her if she were sick as I got the "death look" with her eyes searing into my countenance. I even recall the very first service where I went by myself in an evening Lenten worship. A friend and I, both age 5, sat together in a slick, varnished wooden pew. When the lights went down for the sermon, and the pulpit was spotlighted, we got at opposite ends of the pew on our bellies and pushed off. We cracked heads in the middle, giggled and backed up to do it again until an usher appeared and straightened us out. In later years, I would think of ushers as the "Stormtroopers" of churches. I think it was a few more years before I could "solo" my church attendance. I once compared notes with an older cousin who was also a PK. His Dad used to call ushers by name who would receive the offering each Sunday. One day he called on Bill to come forward and little Billy dutifully went up while the big "Bill" sat back down. Billy took the offering plates and knew just how to pass them down the pews until one person had no offering. Billy glared at their omission commanding them to, "put something in." No stewardship motivation has ever been more direct.

Speaking of ushers, I remember in East Tennessee one Sunday, my sister asked Mom if she could hold her hat after church. It was sort of a beret style hat. She went outside with it where some men stood in a circle chatting and as she went into the circle, she announced that it was her birthday, and she would like them to contribute some change for her. She collected some pocket change. She learned how to be an usher, but the parental reprimand was swift.

I also can recall around age 4, an evening Lenten service sitting in a church pew and observing a man in front of me, and in the middle of his bald head was an awful-looking huge wart so I thankfully did *whisper* in my Mom's ear: "Why does that man have an apple growing out of this head?" In sign language I learned that one finger across lips means "shut up."

In my mature years, I was attending a synod assembly at Roanoke College, dressed, of course, in distinguished clergy garb, and moving through a cafeteria line. A lady behind me said, "are you Jimmy Cobb?" I admitted as much. She said, "I will never forget the time you got away from your Mom after church, stood on the outside column of the church steps and peed into the wind!" (Rader Lutheran, Timberville, VA). Though I had no memory of said crime, (and it was not continued in family folklore), I am sure my red blush admitted to a long buried "fault, a most grievous fault." Yep, confession language after a reliable eye-witness account.

I grew up with two sisters, one, two years younger (the rival) and one, four years younger (the baby). I considered both tolerable annoyances. With Kathy, the middle child, I scoped her out as the competition. Early on, I unknowingly tried to do away with her. As an infant, someone had given her a "baby ring," as a present. I thought if it was hers, she should have it. I delivered her present, she ate it, choked and got the immediate attention of the parents who came running to turn her upside down and luckily, it rolled out. Another time, while the lawn was being mowed and I was pushing her in a swing, I wondered how close I could get her to the lawn mower on the next pass. I got her fairly close, just close enough to the lawn mower's hot exhaust pipe. She has that burn scar on her knee to this day. One other mention: She insisted on traveling downhill in the red Ryder wagon. I thought she was going too fast and I happened to have a broom handle with me to apply a break under the wheel. It slowed her down ok. But the wagon handle flipped up and caught her under the eye. (Yep, another scar under the eye to this day.) And just so you know, she is yet living to a good number of years, healthy and hopefully forgiving.

With "baby" sister, I never had such adventures. Mostly, she requested my help because the refrigerator handle was too high for her to reach. Her litany was "Jimmy, open frig-ater please." I was happy to reveal the source of all food and good things, and the higher shelves were out of her reach anyway where I staked my claim.

I remember Mom tried to be strict about afternoon nap time. I learned to sneak to the back screen door and undo the eyehook to get to the great outdoors. So, they moved the eye hook higher, out of my reach. No problem, that handy broom handle did the trick again. Born free! I remember disliking afternoon naps when Mom and the two girls went into twin beds; I had better things to do. One day the "baby" came out to say she wasn't sleepy. I told her a better bed would be in the bottom bureau drawer with a blanket like a nest. We quietly assembled at the new nap place, she got in and over the bureau went, luckily to be caught by the twin bed with no injury to anyone but the big bang that ended that nap session.

Out behind the house was a huge field. My Dad had the bad habit of burning paper products in a pile out back. One fall day, I came back in saying it was really hot outside. "How can it be hot?" my Mom asked.

For a second time I repeated "it's hot outside." "How can it be hot outside?" she asked. Then she glanced out the kitchen window to see the whole field was on fire. Fire trucks came and it was a great exciting adventure.

First grade was also my first stage debut. Having an audience's attention was intoxicating and led to later years in high school drama. I played Ducky Lucky in the "Henny Penny" barnyard story about the sky falling down. It would later be reflected upon as what can happen when a pernicious rumor circulates (or big lies and media dis-information!) How contemporary was that?

I recite some of these early adventures because they make the case for "original sin." As one commentator put it, "this is the one doctrine of the Christian faith that begs for no more evidence," or as Mark Twain put it: "Humans are the only creature who blush . . . or need to."

CHAPTER 3

Thankful for Faith Formation

PARENTS AND OTHER "CHURCHED" adults have so much influence in the imprinting of the faith. It never comes in one dose but in thousands of examples and illustrations over time. For many Christians, the faith is a matter of accumulated, persistent "wraparounds" of love. How glibly we say, "God is love." We are gifted with food, clothing, shelter and hopefully, a parent or parents or other adults who simply care! The strength of the church is that it is a community, and it is intergenerational.

First, there are the stories and songs. When you grow up as a "PK" (preacher's kid), the imprinting (or is it indoctrination?) is thoroughly applied. Promotions through military ranks have nothing on the ladder climbing in church Christmas pageants. Year after year you progress from a cow (age 3) to a sheep (age 4) to a shepherd (5–8) to an innkeeper, to three or more kings and, if you make the big time, Joseph for males and Mary for females. That's the way it was and forever shall be! (If you should want a special look into the most delightful chronicle, try the one entitled "The Best Christmas Pageant Ever," by Barbara Robinson, also a Hallmark TV special). Many of the pageants happened just the way she told it. Shepherds do bang hockey sticks, angels do fight over haloes and wise men ought to have brought casseroles, diapers, and gift cards. But the main point is that the Jesus story of birth is pondered for every Christmas forever after. And woe to the church that tries to tell it in some other way! You've got the story by age 5 and most of the songs too. Christmas immerses us in memories that are re-presented year after year, and this is the one story that we can all tell with as many unique embellishments as do the two Gospels who conflate it for us.

Other memories continue as well. I remember a children's illustrated Bible and bedtime meant a story with pictures up until I could read myself to sleep. I was drawn to the creation story with a God-like face "blowing" the waters toward the land masses in the early eons toward Eden's garden. I was fascinated with pictures of Noah's ark and all the animals (as are most children); with Moses and two slates of writings coming down the mountain; with boy David and his bravery and courage slaying the giant Goliath with his leather sling shot and taking on a vicious lion (couldn't wait to get my hands on one of those sling shots); and for a dash of danger: Daniel standing in the midst of lions. God was the protector no matter what; these ancient stories said so.

Sunday school openings had everyone singing "Jesus Loves Me This I Know," and there was a Bible verse and pennies brought forward by any "birthday boy or girl," deposited into a church piggy bank for overseas missionaries. Bedtime songs included "Jesus Loves the Little Children, All the Children of the World," and through the more recent civil rights protests, no song encouraged equality and justice for a child more than God's inclusive love of all children with the words "red and yellow, black and white, they are precious in his sight."

I am thankful for each and every teacher who devoted an hour of Sunday School teaching us recalcitrant kids. I am glad that Ms. Hartman wasn't put off or embarrassed when I asked "what is adultery?" and another kid answered, "it's what adults do."

At age 10, some of this stuff got very real for me. We got a call that my grandfather had died and we journeyed to a small town in North Carolina for my first funeral. My Dad had seven siblings and I first thought it was a great family vacation to see all the cousins, aunts and uncles in one place. Sadness came when some of the adults cried and I had not seen that before. I think sadness was there for me when I realized that dying meant we would not see Paw Paw again. I remember standing at the kitchen sink helping Aunt Mildred to dry dishes and daring to venture into a question, "why do these things happen?" She was so natural and matter-of-fact with her reply that no fear was communicated but just a natural progression from life to death that I am grateful to her to this very day that she would not side-step the matter or wallow in grief but said we would thank God for his life in the funeral worship. And we did. And then we cousins went out to play.

When our children were around 7 and 12 years old, we were in the car together for an ice cream outing when I suggested we first stop by a funeral home for a parishioner's visitation for a deceased family member. On the spur, I thought the children ought to experience a funeral home before it was someone in the family when natural grief would take over. We were there only for a few minutes of condolences before they were back in the car. But they had experienced a casket, seen a dead body and heard their parents express sympathy to a family. Both adult sons still tell how their parents took them to see a dead body before ice cream while expressing how none of their friends' families would do this kind of thing. With our beautiful liturgical worship, I do believe that children of a certain age should experience a memorial or funeral service when they are not directly involved in order to prepare them for the inevitable as they may not have an Aunt Mildred to steady their questions. In the meantime, the church's Sunday liturgy parallels the wonderful funeral liturgies and ought to seem natural and predictable.

While we spent my 3rd-5th grade in a small Tennessee town at the foothills of Appalachia, Dad's next call took us to a mid-sized city in Roanoke, VA, 6th grade through high school (1958–65). I loved this place. It had been hard to ride a bike in grass and loose gravel. But now the city had smooth sidewalks like interstate highways for bikes. It had been difficult to visit school friends in rural small towns because of the dispersal across farms and someone might not be able to play due to baling hay or working in a dairy. But moving to the city seemed to present unlimited entertainment: classmates who lived in your neighborhood, music and drama in schools, kickball at recess, school lunches and the big thing eventually was sandlot football. It's a truly by-gone era when one remembers how the church was reinforced by school practices like homeroom readings from Scripture, with prayers and the pledge of allegiance. The assumption was that all were Christians and the pledge mentioned God so the flag and cross were compatible. (Distinguishing the two would become an adult matter.) The Chorus in 6th grade and the choir in junior high school sang hymns and anthems in public performances. No one raised a question about religious tolerance of other faiths or no faith. We had assumptions: all were like us, white, Christian, and middle class. The world was about to change.

CHAPTER 4

Urban and Rural

A Contrasted Life

Knoxville, Tennessee (1954) had only a brief exposure to a large, metro, university city. In that year, some interesting things happened. Our family got its first TV (brand name: Arvin) and our first freezer (brand name Amana, which remained in service from 1955 to 2019!) I saw my first college football game (TN vs KY) in a pouring rain after which my Mom got pleurisy (but I was hooked on football.) I idolized an older teen church member who played high school football and who would go on to West Point. Church consisted of a "mission" congregation getting started in a lodge hall. My chores in this second-grade year meant setting up a card table as an altar and folding chairs for the parishioners and folding bulletins and polishing shoes.

Moving from Knoxville to Blountville meant an antenna for TV had to go on the roof to replace dog ears. In Knoxville, we could see three networks; in rural East Tennessee, maybe two with a "snowy" screen. The networks signed off at night. One favorite kids' show was "Winky Dink" and in each episode you were supposed to send away for a decoder kit with a plastic sheet on the TV and an erasable crayon to follow the squiggly worm until the whole picture was revealed. For those of us without money to purchase the kit, our normal crayons smeared the TV screen and permanently waxed them where no cleaning effort could take away the smear.

Moving to east Tennessee, I remember the celebration of the Salk vaccine as a wondrous eradication of polio. I remember being herded through a mobile trailer in a long line of children to receive the shots. I look back to that time, knowing that I have my first memories of rural poverty: jeans were not fashion statements, but farm-wear only (most always faded and torn.) Children sometimes had a quarter for a school lunch and the poorer ones brought a paper sack with not much in them. Children in school came with holes in shirts, often barefoot and with questionable shoes in winter. In retrospect, I can reflect that a local dentist may not have been at the top of his class since he pulled some of my lower permanent teeth at age 9 resulting in some problems for the rest of my life. The term "food desert" may trace its origin to rural folks having to travel to larger towns for groceries. Nothing seemed to be "at hand" in those days.

The kids in town participated in Little League baseball. My Dad was a leader in the Ruritan Club attempting to get into the town league from our rural outpost. The team was permitted entry and the Central Heights White Sox were ready to go. The season kicked off with the two new entries playing each other. It was 0-0 in the last inning when I lined a double to the fence. Rounding second base toward third, the ball came to the infield and conked me on the head. I went down and came to with Mom and Dad hovering over me. "I'm ok, dusted off jeans (our new uniforms had not arrived yet), scored when the next batter hit a single and we triumphed 1-0 in our baseball debut. Other rural past-times included BB guns and hunting water moccasins down by the creek. (Never killed one, but had some near misses!)

Davy Crockett, the movie, came to Bristol theaters and the first Disney "mass merchandising" campaigns arrived. Every kid needed a coonskin cap and leather vest and of course a BB gun sufficed for a musket.

Besides poverty and lessons in scarcity, I was to learn something too of a reverse "gender" lesson as well (only in hindsight). My Mom and a friend from church decided that her daughter and I ought to sing a duet in the up-coming P.T.A. talent show. We did. We won. But they had never had a boy enter. My prize: a bottle of perfume which I considered humiliating. So, the city seemed like a panacea for escaping some of the confining issues. On to Roanoke, Virginia and the experience of a "big" city (1958–65).

CHAPTER 5

Beginning of Life Discernment
of Right and Wrong

WHILE MANY FRIENDSHIPS IN elementary school had already been set by students who had been there the whole time, the opportunity for several elementary schools to channel into one junior high was a great equalizer for a newcomer like me. Changing classes, having various teachers, having lockers, etc., all became this new world of the next three years' existence. Early school assemblies had the student body president emceeing and introducing the events and I coveted that role by ninth grade. It was the beginning of academics and school politics in a weird combo of ambition. I was a home room rep. to the student council. The ninth-grade head cheerleader said she would be my campaign manager if I ran for treasurer at the end of the 7th grade. She brought some folks together for a Saturday production of posters and the campaign began and drove to a successful election. Candidates made speeches. I was hooked. Student council meetings began to exercise introductions to parliamentary procedure and some of the school's business seemed to encourage the ideas of students. We advised on some policies, recommended school assembly programs, arranged dances and coordinated fund raisers. I found that if you really did work hard you received both teacher affirmation and appreciation from students who trusted you to bring forth good things. Obvious progression: student body president in ninth grade. During junior high years, my Mom was the reader of my papers and I was introduced to the term "pop quizzes." So almost nightly, she would stand at either the sink or the ironing board to quiz me for the next day's subjects.

A societal issue began to appear. The question of race came to the forefront of both church and school. News headlines found that black people were having small delegations attend some "white" churches to see about their reception. Some churches had ushers bar the entrances to worship. My Dad had an ushers' meeting and said that anyone wishing to worship would be warmly welcomed and seated in front pews. The hospitality was to be gracious no matter what. No confrontation would become a tactic. This was not some great social statement; it was simply a practical means to avoid confrontation. In our small parish, such a visit never occurred. Then came the integration of our junior high. I only recall TV cameras on the sidewalk to cover the historic event. Two girls would enter Monroe Junior High (1962). I honestly never knew what the big deal was about that event. Only two remembrances come to mind: At one of the school dances, I heard a rumor that someone would object to their attendance. I thought I had a responsibility to say something. Tim was a big guy, I was small. He had kind of a loud mouth about things. As the two arrived, he jeered at them and I stood in front of him to simply say, "Knock it off. They have a right to be here." The moment passed with no other occurrence. The other noticeable reaction came within the next year when two doctors and a businessman in our neighborhood (and three classmates of mine) moved from Northwest Roanoke to Southwest Roanoke. I did not know why they had gone but later it would be called "white flight."

My Mom had grown up in Columbia, South Carolina, and my grandmother and an aunt next door had black maids or as they say, some "help." Both Victoria and Marie were there 5 days a week and seemed to run the households. At least for us children, through those years, these "colored" women were persons of worth and dignity. Children do not know what underlies the social structures or customs in the old South, but I really think that we saw their humanity and compassion, work ethic and civility even if it was forced into structures we did not comprehend. Both church and school response to integration seemed to say "so what"..., at least in our family unit. We seemed to be brought up with an equality of humanity. Every person has brains and gifts and worth. That's what we knew in our childish naivete. I heard the "n" word from an occasional Carolina relative or visitor but thankfully, not often, and never from my parents. Cursing, labels and "put downs" were considered an 11th commandment "thou shalt not," and were just not allowed. Basically, the message was "any derogatory language is not permitted." An additional memory around seventh grade: there was a hymn in church that was sometimes sung and one of the lines bothered me; it said, "go spread your trophies at his feet" ("All Hail the Power of Jesus' Name," v. 5) and at the 7th grade level, I didn't have any. A motivation to get some was about to unfold.

To see the "other" side of the "real" world, and away from a protective family unit, came from a strange place. A city police officer and his family lived across the street. As I showed interest in football, (throwing passes with neighbor kids in the street), he asked if, instead of playing for a close-by Villa Heights team, if I would consider playing for the Fraternal Order of Police squad. It took special effort for my Dad to agree to transport me to a center city park for daily fall practices. What I did not know was that the police sponsored team was mostly made up of juvenile delinquents referred by police or mandated by the courts! Now I would be exposed to quite different words, phrases and behaviors. I considered it a victory over temptation never to succumb to prohibited language/behaviors. I think the police were glad to have a less troublesome kid on the roster. We had two good police coaches and a father of one of the kids who volunteered his time. My parents were always supportive of my endeavors and I remember one game where the play veered out of bounds and when the tangle of players un-piled, my Mom was on the bottom of the heap, more bruised than any of the players. At the end of three years, we went to the city championship game, held in Victory stadium and broadcast on local TV station WSLS. We lost to a team we had defeated during the regular season mainly because our star fullback failed to make the weigh-in for the 115 lb. limit. I would not realize in hindsight that my across the street police neighbor would become chief of police for Roanoke City and the team coach would become chief of police for neighboring Salem, VA. Two outstanding officers that I had admired for their good influences. I once asked the coach why he had chosen me to play quarterback and he replied that I had a good arm and was the only one on the team who could learn the plays! Sometimes, a teammate would need a ride home and I saw that some lived in some really questionable housing, the type that might receive church Thanksgiving baskets. Yet another brush with what the word "underprivileged" meant, correlating it all to clothing, shelter, food, education and the very lack of parental guidance.

Junior High years meant a lot of firsts: first dance, first date; and, in church, first communion, just after confirmation. Watch out for kids in their first communions: the wafer floats to the top of the mouth and the sip of wine causes every child to cough or worse, gag but it was seen as a passage point in church progression. Having been elected Student Council president, the junior high principal nominated me for a "Hi-Y" leadership week in Black Mountain, NC. Numbers of youth from all other the southeast came to that week to learn about parliamentary procedure, committee organizations and to scope out the other sex for the end of the week dance. I met the son of Tennessee's governor and was impressed that I recognized his last name as a Nashville kid. I was a church rep. to our youth group's annual assembly held one summer at James Madison University (then "Madison College") and later summers at the Lutheran affiliated Roanoke College. I would also soon be elected member-at-large on the Virginia "Luther League" Executive Committee and began to see how training in the school arena and the church arena reinforced each other. These two leadership tracks would be hugely influential in years to come. As ninth grade came to an end, I received the "most outstanding student," award with news pictures, etc., most valuable player on the F.O.P football team and an office in Virginia Luther League so the ego was massaged with a growing appetite for ambition! There were two other growth areas: little tolerance for others who would not put in work to make things happen and a developing sense of right and wrong whether from the brush with issues of integration and civil rights or political issues that seemed to beg for commentary, even from us early teens since we were the source of all knowledge. The political interest was fueled by an 8th grade class trip to D.C. On the basis of what I saw, I decided I would be a lawyer as an entree into the F.B.I. and possibly politics. That would be the goal, all the way into college. (But, in the meantime at least, I had begun to collect some trophies and so fulfill the hymn's verse 5!)

I recall one summer when a vacant church in Virginia Beach asked any pastors who might be interested to come for a week, stay in the vacant parsonage and conduct services on Sunday. Dad decided to sacrifice a Sunday off in order to take our family there for the beach week. The church sat directly on the boardwalk. The building was not air conditioned, so all windows and doors were open. I noticed my Dad stumbling a bit in sermon delivery and I asked him about it later. He said it was a great distraction to see bikinis pass in review looking directly out on the boardwalk. He said even more distracting was the summer wear that some wore as they came to kneel at the communion rail. He admitted to dropping a communion wafer into a woman' cleavage. I asked what he did and he replied, "I couldn't very well retrieve it; she got a second wafer." A fitting improvisation! Early on, the church provided a sense of humor.

Before continuing, I wish to remember our family vacations. Given the extended families (Mom was one of eight children, Dad, one of eight), our family vacations nearly always meant trips to grandparents and occasionally aunts or uncles. This was a special treat for us because numbers of cousins seem to be around with fun things to do: taking a turn at churning home-made ice cream;

finding boiled peanuts or ice-cold watermelons as treats, swimming at pools or day trips to lakes or beaches, Mom's side of the family seemed more relational, casual, easy-going, with people popping in and out the back door for visits. Dad's family seemed more up-tight, academic and in some ways, competitive. Both sets of grandparents seemed welcoming to see us and welcomed our visits usually Thanksgiving, post-Christmas, post-Easter and summers. All first cousins seemed excited for adventures whenever we appeared. Both sides were Lutheran and no Sunday worship was ever missed in any of the homes. Church was thus re-enforced wherever and whenever we visited. By the way, the grandparents, aunts and uncles were great cooks, all of them, across the board. They had a penchant for fried foods: chicken, fish, beer battered hushpuppies, all sorts of barbecue and to this day, I remain a fried food and barbecue aficionado! Vacations represented special re-union times and gave a family solidarity across the generations that meant much to us kids.

CHAPTER 6

The Indelible Imprinting of Senior High (1963–65)

THE INCREDIBLE EXCITEMENT OF growing up into senior high was an adrenaline rush. Now came the confluence of two large junior high schools into one wonderful, newly built campus. It was only the second year of the newly constructed "campus concept" high school. It would win a national architectural award. A central administration building, a stage/cafeteria, a large gym, athletic fields, parking lot, three halls each with a "dean," covered walkways, everything on ground floors. Let the good times roll! Algebra and geometry: not so great. But a love of history, government, English, Latin, etc. foreordained the track to liberal arts. Then came an introduction to the famed director of stage and drama; one Genevieve Dickinson. She was a whirlwind of energy. This red-haired matron of local fame was a force. Her only daughter would grow up to win a national oratorical contest and would marry a would-be writer who would, one day, deliver scripts to Lucille Ball, Danny Kaye and others in Hollywood. In the meantime, to enter into her elective class was to soon be captured in the web of work and fun. Somehow, she grabbed potential talent and I was enthralled to be tapped. That first year I was in two major productions and another smaller play. She groomed one 10th grader for speech contests and sent me on into state finals in the Optimist Oratorical contest. I lost at that level but gained so much experience. I was elected class president for the next three years. I also tasted defeat, losing student body president to a three star, All State athlete by one vote. One classmate said, "I voted for *him* so you could stay class president and head up the junior-senior prom." It did not feel like a good consolation prize. "Politics" could be elation in victory or crushing in defeat. With Ms. "D's" coaching, I would win the American Legion's State of Virginia Oratorical contest (but lose in the four-state regional) and place second in the VFW's "Voice of Democracy' ' contest in Virginia. A lifelong friend, Bill Coulter and I would team up to be finalists for three years in a district forensic debate competition. (Bill would be an English Ph.D. via UVA and Princeton and teach at Randolph Macon Women's College). He was a close neighbor, his father was a high school principal and an excellent, no nonsense administrator. When Bill and I would double date, he would have us come by for ice cream. He once asked what I planned to do and I said "be a lawyer." He asked why. I said, "to make lots of money." He answered, "I hope you would never choose a vocation based on money." That comment stuck. Ms. June Webb would direct a large and talented choir and we would cap our senior year with a concert performance at National Cathedral in Washington D.C. I was honored to be chosen to attend the American Legion's "Boys State" experience held on the campus of the College of William and Mary. I would write home and say, "this is where I want to go to college." I attempted to gain an appointment as a congressional page with the endorsement of a Roanoke state senator and a local judge but no one in the Virginia delegation had that appointment during my application year.

Senior High was the place of many friendships and experiences. Some retain negative memories but I only have positive ones. Around 9th or 10th grade, my Dad handed me a book that was supposed to answer questions about the anatomy of sex. It was entitled, "Into Manhood." He said, "if you have any questions, ask." I read the book; it left many things unexplained even to the imagination but I never brought up the subject. One morning in 10th grade, we left early, went to a grocery store parking lot for the first driving lesson. That felt like a moment of maturity. The real lesson would be driver's ed. with the high school football coach as teacher. How we didn't crash the car, I'll never know. The class used a 63' Chevy Biscayne. After the lessons, the parents needed a new car and it would be a white, 1963 Chevy Biscayne. Then came the Learners' permit, finally, the license! Since there was only one car in the family, I would have to arrange schedules for Friday night dates. Those two matters led to a remembrance of the first romance. She (Fran was her name) and I dated mostly through the three years with occasions of break-ups and then other dates as well. In the school theater world, the first dance was called the "Snowball Dance," semi-formal. Fran accepted my invitation. Thus, there was the teen experience of falling in love and then out of love. It becomes one of those lifelong "sorting" times when you begin to discover who you might really attach to in serious later years. We were in a drama together, also in choir. In government class, we had our dean, Jack Graybill, who would challenge students' various perspectives on how to think and why. We would argue conservative and liberal cases around any issue. My "date" was always into the arguments with him and I was impressed. Once in class, he asserted that he wished to be able to pay more taxes. The debate was around "why?" My teen years were immersed in conservative thinking. I was elected Vice President of the Roanoke teenage Republicans. My Dad took Coulter and me out of school one day to hear Barry Goldwater (Fall, 1964) speak at an airport in Tri-Cities, Tennessee. (Today, it's such an embarrassing memory as college study would send me into a 180 turn-around!) This conservative teen was living just before all revolutions: cultural, political, institutional, sexual, etc. Even that first kiss was cautious and careful. Remember: no bad language, certainly no alcohol, drugs or sex. Meanwhile back at church. Those Luther League officers continued to be influential. I would be elected President of the Virginia Synod Luther League and onto the national board of the church's youth organization. I attended a regional youth assembly in Myrtle Beach, SC and one of the speakers was William String-fellow, a Harvard law grad and a stellar Christian who dedicated his practice to under-served victims from his office in Harlem, NY. Later, I attended a regional youth gathering in NC and the theme was on "race relations." There was a courageous panel of pastors addressing the issue. One in particular had lost half of his congregation over the issue. We were divided into small groups to talk about Scriptural and historical backgrounds of how segregation could persist. Our small group leader was a student at Harvard and I was impressed. He asked if I could be a scribe for the small group and report to the larger assembly later and if I needed help, a small group would gather later to compose a summary. I listened to group reflections and by the end of the session turned in a summary paper entitled "An Open Letter to Those Who Love." The group heard it and said it captured the group's thoughts. It was later published via the national Luther League's response to the topic. (Years later, I would discover it in a bound volume in a seminary library; I wish I had a copy but I do not.)

One of the speakers at the assembly was a black pastor who served on the Church's national staff in New York. He stayed in a dorm room where we were all housed. In the evening, some of the teens donned a bed sheet and came toward him in the hallway making ghost-like sounds. Since this was a supposed prank by some mimicking the KKK, I was disgusted that the topic, the theme, the speakers, and the workshops, etc., had so little impact on some of these teen's despicable behaviors. It illustrated a racial disconnect between a hoped for future and present day reality. It was a memorable lesson with both negative and positive recall. I was elected to the national convention in Miami and that involved my first airplane ride to a major city. Following that convention, I would be elected to attend the national convention in Milwaukee and would be elected to the national Luther League board. In a "social conscience" framework, we decided to disband the youth auxiliary for two reasons: money could be spent in better ways for social causes and we wanted to challenge our congregations and national church to include us in the fulness of church leadership (e.g. local church councils, etc.) It was probably not a good move and in hindsight, I regret it.

One memorable day in high school, my across-the-street police neighbor (the instigator of my sandlot career) called me over one Sunday to say that he had been doing yard work all day and saw me go out four times: one time I was dressed in shirt and tie. I said, "Yes, that was for my newspaper sports column writing downtown." Then, you went out in a fairy costume, "Yes, that was to go to a TV studio for a one act televised play called "Poor Maddalena." Then you went out in jeans and a butterfly net and a bucket. "Yes, that was to do a field quadrant sweep for a Biology assignment." Then you went out in a sheet! "Yes, that was for the Latin banquet." He remarked that I had had a full day. Indeed!

Speaking of my newspaper job, remember the team where we lost the city championship? It was coached by Roanoke World News editor Bob McClelland. He hired me my senior year to write sports for the newspaper and assigned me through the year to cover high school games in football and basketball. I had to write the column and be at the sports desk at 5 AM to put the writing to bed by 10:30. I loved the experience. By season's end, they sent me to the lofty heights of Virginia Tech's coliseum for an assignment! I was thrilled. That first job was a "connector" moment to previous football encounters and "connections" would seem to follow me through life!

In the late fall of senior year (1965), I received early admission to my first college choice: The College of William and Mary. I would enter as a pre-law student and prepare for a legal career. As a history major intent on the study of colonial history with all those influential Virginians once in the student body, I was thrilled to be immersed in the town, its history and possibilities.

CHAPTER 7

Academic Imprinting for Life

I DID NOT KNOW that going to college meant that I would take my whole family with me! Dad accepted a call to Norge, VA, just outside Williamsburg and therefore I would be a day student instead of a dorm resident. At the time, and in retrospect, I knew money was an issue but also to this day, I realize how much of the true college experience I missed. Three very close friends from Roanoke would also be joining me in Williamsburg and we mostly stayed in touch through those times. Two of my first outlets for college extra-curricular interests were again, school and church, namely, the college debate team and Lutheran Student Association at St. Stephen, across from campus with its Sunday evening meals and chats. It was a time of civil rights and Vietnam issues, particularly on college campuses. I was in ROTC for two years before dropping the course on the way to what I thought would be law school. Collegiate debating seemed like a natural progression from debate in high school. I traveled to various "meets" with the team; most notably Wake Forest, where I ran into my first cousin who was there with another college. We did not compete against each other but it was a treat to see each other. At the end of freshman year, the faculty sponsor put me with a senior in order to debate two visiting guests from Cambridge Univ. in a large, packed public hall. It was enjoyable to again be "on stage," but I decided after that year not to continue in debate because the work was huge (the equivalent, I think, of two academic courses). That year, I declared history as my major.

During the first two years of college, I supported my tuition, fees, car and gas first, though speech contest earnings in high school and second, through a part-time job as a costumed interpreter at Jamestown Festival Park. I rotated assignments between the fort and the three ships; I had to learn Jamestown history and speak it to crowds of tourists, through the year. Winter outside was cold and bleak but framed the imagination with how the first English settlers had to cope. One unforgettable moment was the filming of a "travelogue" when we stood around an open grave depicting the starvation winter of 1609–10. We "settlers" lowered a log between two blankets into the grave. The Director yelled, "cut . . . that looks like a log, we need a body." He looked around the circle, pointed to me and said, "you'll do." So, down into the grave I went! Shovels of dirt were thrown in until that part of the film ended and then I came up and out of the grave! That experience would later preach!

By year three, I worked in the Dean of Men's office in clerking and odd jobs. In each of the years that Virginia Boys' State was held on campus, I was invited to deliver my Virginia Oratorical Speech that had won the American Legion state contest. Then, once again, a coincidental connection appeared. The assistant Dean, (named Wallace Elliott) had been a football coach in Roanoke. In my interview he said, "did you write sports for the newspaper? "I did." He said, "I remember when you first were on the sidelines and identified yourself as the writer for the game, I thought, "the sports staff has sunk to new lows, sending a high schooler to cover the game." But after the article, he said, "after your coverage, I called and requested you because you quoted me accurately. I considered you the first to do so. Welcome to this office." Such coincidences seem to follow me for my lifetime. Someone wrote "coincidences are God's way of going anonymous." There are many of those still to come. Though I had kind of cruised through high school, I found college to be a tester and knock me off my lofty perch. I was shaken to receive my first C and an unthinkable D in that freshman year (mostly due to geology, I could never identify striations in rocks!). The rest of the way improved with solid B's and an occasional A, all the way to consistent Dean's List standing. My drama/ speech teacher followed me in two ways to Williamsburg. One of her star students had opened a dinner theater in Toano, VA and she paved the way for me to get a job with a musical production. After one day, I quit (the one and only job I ever quit). I was exhausted, every part of my body ached after one day and I had no rhythm at all! Second, Ms. "D" had sent in my oratorical speech to the Valley Forge Freedoms' Foundation and it was awarded an honorable mention which seemed to be a big deal to the college newspaper. Two serious dating relationships occurred in the college years. Alice was a bright (Phi Beta Kappa) Lutheran whom I met in L.S.A. She would later go on to Lutheran School of Theology in Chicago and become a Pastor. But we broke up my junior year. Then I dated an Overland Park Kansas coed whom I also met in L.S.A. Since she was two years younger, the relationship did not survive my departure to seminary.

Some college faculty made lasting impressions in different ways. There were some outstanding teachers in history, psychology, education, philosophy, English. The College had a combined six-year B.A. and law degree and therefore, I had a law professor as my advisor. In my junior year, he and I had a significant conversation. The college decided to take religion courses out of philosophy and make it a separate department. They brought in two outstanding profs. to teach. I was attracted to a course entitled, "Contemporary Christian Theology." It would be taught by a dynamic professor named James Livingston. His lectures to us became the basis of a MacMillan textbook by the same name. I went in to get my law professor's approval and he asked, "why would you want to waste your time with a religion course?" He said, "you must be churched or something; which one?" "Lutheran," I said. He followed "I don't like Lutherans." "Why?" I asked. "Because they do that confession thing at the beginning and it deflates the noble human spirit." We proceeded to engage in an hour-long discussion on the nature of confession. (I think I held my own with this legal scholar.) At the end, he said, "I guess I need to sign your course card." "If you do, I'm out of here, thank you." I did not know how prophetic my exit would become.

Those first two courses (adding another entitled, "Religious History in America," by Dr. David Holmes) were formative. Most students have to give up Sunday School superficial stories and find a deeper or more substantive understanding of deeper theology. I would have two huge teaching giants for that guidance (Livingston and Holmes who remained lifelong friends.) I shall always be appreciative.

At the same time, the campus pastor, Dr. John Byerly, was a devotee of Dietrich Bonhoeffer's life and times. He also brought to the L.S.A. a movie entitled "A Time for Burning," about a young Lutheran pastor in Omaha, NE, who was probing race relations in his city. The documentary was honest and truthful. At that time, I had a professor teaching Sociology of Religion (Dr. Elaine Themo) and suggested that she must see this film. She did and brought it forward to the classroom. Again, school and church seemed to have an on-going dialogue with each other. One of my most influential history profs. was Dr. Richard Sherman whose lectures on economics and history turned my thinking from conservative to liberal about many on-going social issues. It was conversion time for me. I also admired him for standing with others on the walkway to the student union building during lunch hour in silent protest of the war in Vietnam. During that time, my home church in Norge, VA had a small adult forum where the teacher often asked me to lead and comment on current events and social issues and my anti-war bias took the form not of protests, but of teaching. Perhaps my Lutheran quietism was too deeply embedded for protest lines and signs in those years.

Also, while a student, I remember attending the state convention of the NAACP in Williamsburg. I was one of only a few whites in the audience and it would always be good to experience being in a minority group now and then just for the dynamic reversal of the feeling.

Somewhere in the college timeline, I went for a visit with the President (now the nomenclature is "bishop") of the Virginia Lutheran Synod. I told him I was interested in at least a year in seminary to explore course work and vocation. My campus pastor recommended Chicago among our eight seminaries. He said the most urban seminary was the place to study. Many in my family had attended Southern Seminary in Columbia, SC and I did not want to go "where others had led the way." But I did say to my campus pastor, "do you know what the three most significant urban pastors in Manhattan, D.C. and Philadelphia all have in common?" "No," he said. "I responded, "they all went to Gettysburg Seminary. That's where I'll go to hang out for at least a year."

College graduation was a nostalgic kind of celebration. One interesting moment: When the line formed for the graduation of Fleming High in Roanoke (with 420 grads), coming from two directions, I was partnered with a classmate, Kay Pulliam. When the line formed for William and Mary's graduation (over 1400), we turned the corner and I met my walking partner, Kay again. What were the odds?

CHAPTER 8

Theology Formation and Some Surprises

FOR THOSE OF US without the study of Greek, a summer six-week prep course was required. It was a joint session with Philadelphia Seminary and bonded the group of about 40 in this summer "boot camp" experience. Gettysburg Seminary boasted one of finest faculties around Lutheran circles: Scholars at Gettysburg included renowned theologian Robert Jensen, Luther/Reformation scholar Eric Gritsch and preaching professor Herman Stuempfle. College academicians had given good prep for these scholars to follow next. Their depth of learning was obvious and they were dedicated to the Church. Originally thinking of one year's trial exploration and possibly moving into a teaching profession, field work requirements were completely geared to parish settings. I had not always enjoyed parish life or being a "PK" (preacher's kid). The field work assignments simply sent us as observers to different settings. I enjoyed a semester at Christ Church, York, PA and Gettysburg College (with two wonderful campus pastors in John Vannorsdall, later to be chaplain at Yale Univ. and then President of Philadelphia Seminary, and Jerry Knoche, later to be campus pastor at the Univ. of WI, Madison, and later, my Bishop in the DEMD Synod). Their enjoyment of parish life was contagious and I was being introduced to different ministerial settings apart from the many quarrels and conflicts that seemed inherent in the DNA of small parishes served by my Dad. At the end of year one, we were assigned to various hospitals around the country for CPE (Clinical Pastoral Education). I went to Richmond (VA) Memorial Hospital and had a very rough instructor whose mission seemed to be to take us apart and hopefully put us back together again. The Freudian "onion peel," was not my favorite time in seminary. It was really hard work in a small group of potential chaplains whose group sessions could be vicious in critique. Each person had at least two or three verbatims (reconstruction of chaplain/patient conversations) that the group would critique. This was followed by case studies that were longer in duration and concluded the summer with a major paper on reflective learning. I remember the first long-term patient I had: a young woman whose husband was in Vietnam; an affair with another man, pregnancy followed by abortion. Her family turned their backs on her except for her mother. The mother was then killed in an auto accident one night driving home from the hospital. This deep guilt of a young woman was clearly moving towards inconsolable depression. I don't think I helped at all except in absorbing the story as a listener. I do remember walking out of the hospital that afternoon and being grateful to feel sunshine and a breeze on my face. I was learning that this pastoral care matter could be hugely and tragically unpredictable. The supervisor at the conclusion of the summer read a part of my paper quoting Bonhoeffer that "some parts of our being are too deep except for God to know." That was my justification for avoiding some of the emotional spillage that others in the group had shown. The supervisor said that if he lived long enough, he expected to read some of my writings since that was my main avenue of expression. Some years later, another supervisory friend asked me who he was and when I said his name and the year involved, she replied, "no wonder he was so hard on you. That was the group he needed for his own supervisory credential." That explained a lot. Upon returning to seminary some 20 classmates had dropped out and several marriages hit the rocks. It was a personality transforming summer, not always for the good. (Over the years, this experience is still needed but has lessened in intensity and is less psychiatric in scope.) I am glad to have survived.

In year two, I had a paid "assistantship" in a Baltimore congregation to be a part of youth ministry. The seminary taught us to preach from the text of a three-year lectionary but this two "older pastor tandem" seemed to ignore the texts, preach on their own selections and alternate 8:30 and 11:00 worship service between themselves and thereby preach half the sermons that a lone parish pastor would! It all added to the irrelevance of the pulpit, or so I thought.

At the end of the second year, we were allowed to select a region to consider our "internship" location. Because I had never been in New England, that was my first choice. I was sent to Tokyo, Japan, for an international experience. Lutherans have a number of English-speaking congregations in various world capitals and this was one. With about 150 congregants, this congregation was vibrant. It was composed of corporate execs from the midwest such as General Foods, 3 M, etc. There were two ambassadors: the U.S. and Madagascar envoys. There were the families of seminary faculty and missionaries in the country. I had an unbelievable, formative year in Japan. I taught confirmation at "Luther Dorm," adjacent to the American School in Japan. I taught a Bible study to Japanese who also wanted to hear and speak English. I met people who knew the work of my great Aunt who established a girls' school in Kumamoto in the 1930's and returned post-World War II to teach there till the end of her career. I learned so much in that intern year: what it meant to be in a "minority" religion in a nation; how money exchanges affected the salaries of clergy and overseas staff; how U.S. national policies were perceived by another country; how different denominations helped one another in that close familial sense of real ecumenism, how military chaplains often supported congregations in expatriate places, how Japanese people were gracious and welcoming to foreigners. There were other lessons as well. The Lutheran Church in Japan seemed to have two strata of members, the poor and outcast and the wealthy and educated. Post-World War II, the church stepped in to serve widows and orphans. In a nation-state that defined itself as "family" with the Son-god emperor at the head, the "judgment" toward widows and orphans resulted in their being cut off from the family due to the death of their husband/father. The second Lutheran Church strata had to do with "elites." That year I met Lutherans who included the head of the Univ. of Tokyo's Medical specialty in ENT; a chief scientist in their space program, a staff aid to Tokyo's governor. Many of these had studied in the U.S. and became leaders in Japanese Lutheran circles.

Two "connector" stories, I will always remember. Once during worship departures, I heard someone say they were from Roanoke, VA. When I went over to introduce myself, it turned out that he was a Marine JAG officer and the brother of the girl I took to the senior prom in high school! Another time, in a coffee hour, I heard the word from a Japanese woman who said, "Lenoir Rhyne College." I had so many aunts, uncles and family who attended that Lutheran College and when I went for that introduction, I found she had been my Aunt's suite-mate in the early 50's. They had lost touch with each other and through me, re-established a friendship.

I am forever grateful to the intern pastor supervisor who guided me through that year especially with a severe sinus/throat infection that led me to the ENT doctor on numerous occasions. I was also glad to be the tour escort for Dr. Oswald Hoffmann who came to Japan as the military chaplains' retreat leader for a week. "Ossie was the renown national radio preacher on the "Lutheran Hour," and seemed to be the very personification of a modern Martin Luther with his storytelling and infectious laugh. As a "Missouri Synod" Lutheran, he invited me to stop in St. Louis and attend a Cardinals baseball game and enjoy a Concordia Seminary tour. He was a personal friend to many seminary and business leaders including the Busch family (as in "Anheuser Busch") whose hospitality suite we enjoyed. I would later see Ossie in Michigan and D.C. several times on his national speaking tours.

The U.S. Ambassador, who was a member of the St. Paul English speaking parish, had two stories he shared: He learned that Nixon would be going to China and he nearly fell out of the barber's chair with that "breaking news" story. Why? Because in the orient, you fore-warn your friend first, not last and you do NOT spring surprises. He knew some repair work would be needed. Second, he oversaw the reversion of Okinawa to Japan; the first-time conquered territory had been returned to an enemy combatant. (This was 1972.) That same year, several different Japanese soldiers came out of Okinawa jungles who had stayed hidden for 27 years since the war's end and had to be slowly re-educated in terms of history and cultural shock that awaited them. What a story and what experiences I absorbed in that intern year in Tokyo. And again, "connections."

Coming back to the states felt joyful and much like a full summer's reunion with extended family, comfort food and welcome home gatherings. I was thankful for what the year had meant. It was the first time I had kept a journal and occasionally I will find the journal and remember the kindnesses of so many mission personnel and parishioners who were such gracious hosts and friends to me.

Soon, it will be fall and a return for senior year in seminary. I secured an assistantship at Gettysburg Presbyterian Church to be a worship assistant and youth teacher with good pay for the effort. It was President Eisenhower's parish and Mamie still worshipped there with a Secret Service attendant. I was invited out to dinner with Ike's cardiologist and wife and he told me that Ike had given him a golf putter that had been written up in Reader's Digest. It had a tape measure, a level, a light for night play and a horn to announce you were about to putt! Fascinating invention. The wife knew I was a Virginian and said, "don't you all just love Robert E. Lee; he was such a gentleman." I replied, "no, I don't admire him at all; he was on the wrong side of history; gentlemanly behavior can't erase a wrong cause." Ouch! Living on the battlefield campus, you soon caught on that one had to advocate truth telling as best you could. The wife suddenly became a more cautious conversational hostess.

One year in seminary we learned that students in a peaceful protest were killed at Kent State University. Our professors led a march from Seminary Ridge to the "Peace Light" on the battlefield in protest. Later, various ones of us proceeded to the march in D.C. that would first convene at New York Avenue Presbyterian Church (the famous church of Senate chaplain, Peter Marshall). I met the church secretary that afternoon and she said, "I don't agree with this gathering, in the meantime, I do my work." I thought of faithful servants who stay at their posts even when it is difficult. The line-up that evening included singer Judy Collins, Sen. Ted Kennedy, Rep. Allan Lowenstein and Yale Chaplain William Sloane Coffin.

That fall, I purchased two tickets for a William and Mary football game without knowing who the second ticket would be for. Entering the first-year class was an attractive, smart, and vivacious student named Judy Dawson. She was a Baltimore native by way of D.C. She had been accepted at Yale Divinity School but worked post-college as an insurance adjuster in Washington, D.C. I was attracted, if not smitten. My line was this: "You're from Baltimore, right? So, you must know how to get to Annapolis right?" She answered, "Yes." "I have two tickets for a Navy football game with my alma mater. Want to go?" That's what started this lifetime marriage adventure. The car ride included singing funny songs all the way to Annapolis and back . We were inseparable in that fall semester. On campus, we played ping pong, attempted tennis, went to the local Diner for bowls of chili, studied together and walked a lot! Then in December we attended an Advent worship where John Vannorsdall preached. He kept asking a question from the Isaiah text: "The grass withers, the flower fades, to whom shall I turn?" Later that evening Judy remembers that the proposal went something like, "if the grass withers and the flowers fade, I would like to turn to you for the rest of my life." When I asked her to marry me, she said "yesterday." I asked, "what does that mean?" (Good Lutheran catechism question), she affirmed a "yes" and since I could then understand the answer, she added, "but I never want to be bored." (We never have been, ever!) We were engaged on Pearl Harbor day and would be married on Armed Forces day. It helps to remember.

Some faculty commented, "Who is this girl who got Cobb out of the library?" She took me home to meet her parents. They served a Baltimore delicacy that I had never seen before: soft-shelled crabs. It looked like a platter of giant spiders. But after asking "What on these seafood things can you eat?" The answer was, "The whole thing." I tried the new dish and loved them. I would soon learn the proper way to open hard-shelled crabs and this new feast has been a lifelong treat. That Halloween, we were in a store at the Gettysburg traffic circle and Judy heard me, in another aisle, talking with someone and I introduced her to Mamie Eisenhower, who was in the store buying candy for her grandchildren. (I had a weekend assistantship at the Presbyterian Church and knew her from there.)

Meeting my parents was a different sort of trip. When asked if she would like some iced tea (around a cold Thanksgiving) she asked if it was sugar free. Wrong assumption, especially when she asked for water instead. That indignity to the southern tradition of sweet tea has long been remembered in family lore. Forever after, this "northern woman in seminary" ("for goodness sake") would stumble over old South customs that put her reputation in jeopardy. On her first visit to my home, there were no guest rooms so she did not know that she would sleep with my sister. For years she had a habit (since she was a baby) of camp-styled crossed legs and totally folding over her body in some type of yoga-like gymnastics flop. Years later, we heard that my sister had whispered to my Mom, "Judy sleeps funny," without knowing what that exactly meant. Once married, this "posture flop" continued all the way through the first baby's birth. The only inconvenience was that the "flop" also took the bed covers with her. Oh well . . .

We decided to get married the day after graduation because the families could be there for both events. So, the graduation took place, and then we ran our own wedding rehearsal (Judy's Dad called her 'sergeant'.) We were to have the reception across the street in the seminary refectory. We had invited 150 guests but with an expandable number: I worked in a church, Judy worked in a church, and I was called to my first parish in Annapolis, Maryland. We had 450 guests show up. The three churches each filled buses and came to campus! One professor had 4 guests from Sweden and he thought it would be fun for them to see an American wedding. We would find out later that the Eucharistic celebration would include the whole congregation with Jewish and Muslim guests going to the table as well! The refectory chef panicked at the miscalculated numbers of guests and began pulling out graduation left-overs and successfully made provisions for the expanded crowd (a true "Jesus-like" feat.) Some interesting moments about the wedding: The preacher was the seminary president; the presider was the Dean, and my Dad led the vows. Judy's grandfather was extremely deaf and had a shirt pocket hearing aid. For some reason, the timbre of the Dean's voice perfectly hit the hearing aid and he heard the liturgy for the first time in some 25 years! Also, Judy's parents' friends were Jewish and from Connecticut. When he stepped into the refectory, he said, "I've been here before." He had been a German national during World War II, got out of Germany and worked for the American army in enemy officer interrogation. Without knowing geography, he was whisked from various prison camps around the country and that very evening found that there had been a German officers' prison at Gettysburg's Camp Colt. With them, he had taken meals in this very refectory, and he had never known where he was. During the reception, my introverted self needed a time apart from the crowds. I was discovered in the kitchen eating brownies with the cook!

Meanwhile, we had little money for a trip but had saved and decided the honeymoon would be spent at Disney World. Judy's grandmother made arrangements for us to stay in her friend's Florida "cottage in the orange grove," on a lake not so far from Orlando. We accepted the gracious offer and made our way south. In my usual romantic ways, the first night included opening envelopes received at the wedding and counting cash gifts to help determine how many days we could spend on the road. Eventually, we arrived in MontVerde, Florida for the "cottage." This trip became so symbolic about how life would be: fun, but a bit off kilter. The "cottage" turned out to be a double bed in the separate garage laundry room with a glass door. The "orange grove" was accurate except that the season was over, no blossoms to be seen; but plenty of smashed, rotting oranges all over the ground. The lake, not so good for swimming, carried a warning, "alligators present." Our hostess was widowed and liked to ask if I could reach some things on her shelves that she had hoped to pull out. If we were around in the late afternoon, the garage bedroom did have a TV to catch the Watergate hearings. We went to Disney World a couple of days, had umbrella drinks at Polynesian Village, carefully donned swimming suits in the restrooms to hit the beach in the afternoon posing as hotel guests. (Sorry about that, Disney.) When returning to our "cottage," I would kill the headlights and coast into the driveway only to hear our hostess call out "yoo-who, Perry Mason is on." One morning she served a quick breakfast and announced that some of her friends would like "pastoral visits." We obliged and made some improvised visits around the lake. She told us that the unofficial "mayor" of Mont Verde was quite the artist. We saw some of her paintings (they were below average), she took us to the basement where she was preparing a canvas and where a "real" artist had drawn pencil sketches and suggested colors! Her art was a hybrid "paint by numbers."

The remainder of our "honeymoon" included visits to relatives in SC and NC in order to arrive at Lenoir-Rhyne College, in the town of my birth. We would see my two sisters graduate from college and then the NC Synod would ordain 16 of us on June 3, 1973. My Dad was looking forward to being asked to preach but that invitation was usurped by a visiting Bishop from Singapore/Malaysia. Dad was a lector and proceeded to read the wrong lesson (guess that would show them!) After the long, long service, I was invited to baptize my sister's new baby, my niece, in a side chapel as my first official pastoral act. My large family unit in attendance gathered round and the saving grace was administered. Through these "testers," we loved each other, and we remembered that, "Love is patient and kind . . . and endures all things." Now it was on to "first call" as Assistant Pastor of St. Martin Lutheran Church in Annapolis, MD.

CHAPTER 9

An Aside about Ruth and Eric Gritsch

THIS COUPLE FOLLOWED US through each of the parishes we served. Whenever I brought forth a "guest theologian" for a weekend of preaching and study, Eric was invited. They came. They were two eccentrics! He was from Austria, she from France. Both were World War II refugees. His father had been a Lutheran pastor in Austria and part of the underground network found Eric (pre-teen) riding a bike past Nazi guards with codes on a church bulletin. He was recruited for Hitler youth only to reject guns and went on to hide in an abandoned tank (and he suffered from claustrophobia for the rest of his life.) She was a child refugee brought to America with a room full of children, some of whom challenged her to go to the head table, with a piece of chicken on a fork and ask, "How do you eat this?" She did. The lady was Eleanor Roosevelt who then took Ruth on a tour to sell war bonds! Post-war, she would work as an office person in a major scholarship foundation. Eric applied and received one for his Ph.D. at Yale in Reformation history. They married; he taught at Wellesley and later they came to the campus of Gettysburg Seminary. I remember in Fredericksburg, VA, the congregational picnic was held on the Rappahannock River and she strolled while holding a lace umbrella as a sun protector. There were comments from the crowd. I remember Eric's visit to us in Grand Rapids, MI and in our home for lunch, Christopher invited him to sit and watch "The Lone Ranger." Later, Eric said he taught Christopher about the masked man being a lot like St. Mark's version of the "messianic secret!" Late in life, sadly, Eric and Ruth divorced. Judy would become her pastor at St. James, Gettysburg, and Eric would remarry, settle in Baltimore and become my close friend/ mentor, again. Such a privilege to know one of the great Luther scholars of all time and his equally brilliant wife!

CHAPTER 10

Thoughts about Parish Ministry

I WANT TO TURN to parish ministry and make some comments about ordained ministry that spans close to 50 years. Thankfully, I will turn to parish remembrances, not to "tell all," but to highlight in each setting something memorable, mostly humorous but also poignant.

Remember that I was very dubious at first that I could serve in parish ministry without having a very positive youthful reflection on small parish life as a "PK." But I was surprised to have such enjoyment in seminary field work, internship, parish jobs, on the way to graduation and Judy and I looked forward to an unfolding adventure in parish ministry. She had a year left to finish her M.A.R. degree. By taking the Annapolis parish, she could finish course work in the Washington Theological Consortium and field work was arranged at the Annapolis Missouri Synod parochial school where she would teach religion to elementary students but would not be allowed to commune due to Lutheran Church-MO Synod policies. (An ironic and later connection story: A member at St. James church in Gettysburg would introduce her visiting father to her and he would receive Communion from her; yes, the same MO Synod pastor whose Annapolis church could not commune her!)

There certainly were first year marriage stresses: my first call, her commuting to classes, our getting to know how each thought and operated. My introversion met her extroversion and later in taking the "Myers-Briggs" personality inventory, we had totally opposite letters in every category! What follows will not be a lengthy treatise on each parish. Rather, I wish to say some things here about parish ministry and then highlight memories of each call, again in humor and poignancy. Now about parish ministry . . .

It is a deep privilege and joy to serve in parish ministry. There is no vocation where you are invited into the interior of people's lives in their deepest times of celebration, grief, and pain, in addition to the ordinariness of routines in living. It is a 24/7 life where a sudden phone call sends you up and out: births, crises, deaths (sudden or long-term lingering anticipation, suicides or accidents.) Expect to have one's "day off" interrupted; expect that vacation times will yet field a crisis call finding you on the beach, in the mountains or out of the country. Count on it!

I found that "normal" routines generally tried to find me in the office in mornings, afternoons in hospitals, nursing homes or homebound visits, and evenings in either church committees or home visits because of parishioner work schedules. Parishioners would sometimes make appointments to stop by or just drop in to see if they might catch you. What was to be done in the mornings? Study of the upcoming lectionary texts for sermon writings, phone calls to return, (from the mid-90's, emails), newsletter articles to write, upcoming Council and committee agenda, bulletin prep, and the occasional funeral or wedding or baptismal visits to convene. Early on, I dropped the phrase pastoral "counseling" not wanting to advertise something that had become rather specialized and credentialed and used the lighter term, pastoral "conversations." Visitation was absolutely crucial for getting to know parishioners in order to establish on-going relationships. In this regard one would learn that there were those in the inner circle who were attracted to the work and mission and your leadership and the outer circle-who were critical, oppositional and stand-offish. Discretion and diplomacy would be necessary additions to the pastor's toolbox.

It is deeply agonizing to serve in parish ministry. There will always be opponents even as there were with Jesus. The pastoral mirror will always reflect right back to you showing the failures, shortcomings and missteps that you recognize daily. There are visits you did not make, cues you missed and assignments you dropped. Your pastoral predecessor will have always succeeded where you failed. If married, your spouse and children will often be disappointed that you messed up a family event because the church called. I will not quote various writers, but I have never found a more descriptive account of parish work than in an article called "Overwhelming Demands," in which Roland Martinson writes:

> Those in the hospital need visits, as do those who are shut-in, dying and bereaved. The chemically dependent, sexually abused, newly divorced, sexually addicted, physically abused and depressed create constant flows of crises requiring immediate attention. Dysfunctional families, troubled marriages and neurotic individuals create havoc in their own lives and that of the congregation. New members need care; so do the parents of the child to be baptized. Those who are engaged require premarital preparation. Young parents need support; so do parents of teenagers, the handicapped and mentally ill. Marriages need enriching; sorrow requires consolation; singles and seniors deserve attention. So do the unemployed, the middle-aged, newly married and the childless. Soon, with evenings already committed to meetings, the days grow too short and double-scheduled nights far too long.
>
> And then there is preaching! There are at least forty-eight Sunday sermons for most pastors. Then come Advent and Lenten services and Holy Week. Sermons must be preached at confirmations, nursing homes, judicatory events, weddings and funerals. Usually a pastor preaches seventy-five to ninety times a year to nearly the same hearers. Pastors are expected to teach. At the least, they are usually responsible for confirmation, a Bible study, and the women's group leaders. In addition, any strong

parish must have adult forums, new members' classes, parenting classes, baptism classes, first communion class, evangelism and social ministry training as well as leadership, spirituality, and intergenerational retreats.

Congregational and judicatory reports require record-keeping, compiling, and framing. Budgets mean data-gathering, assembling, presenting and balancing. There are conflicts between the trustees and the Christian Education committees. Anonymous letters come from those who do not like the preaching or those who say the hymns are too hard to sing or the carpets are the wrong color. Who is going to attend long range planning? The new church council members need orientation. How is all this to be accomplished with too few people and not enough money? Through leadership? There is more needed than a whole team could provide.

The litany could go on still. This beginning recitation simply points to the pressures on pastors to produce. With the pressures come stress. A never-ending stream of demands eats away at the time for preparation, creating mediocrity and ineffectiveness. Renewed efforts and self resolve are difficult to marshal in the face of the resulting loss of worth and confidence. The pain and confusion gnaw at the pastor's spirit, cutting the congregation off from the clergy person's creativity and untapped gifts. Too often the heavy load destroys the pastor's being and personal relationships. Overwhelming demands and ever-increasing expectations constantly undermine ordained ministry. It is not a pretty picture, yet more often than not it is the real one in most pastors' weeks, years or decades in ministry.[1]

A much older evaluative comment from Martin Luther's *Letters of Spiritual Counsel*, hints at the same thing: "the untamed masses are unwilling to be corrected and it is the duty of the preacher to reprove them. This is a very burdensome and perilous duty. And on this account, laymen keep sharp eyes on the clergy. They try to find some fault in them, and if they discover a grievous offense, even if it be the clergy's spouse or children, they are delighted to

1. Martinson, *Called and Ordained*, 181–82.

take their revenge on them . . . Even if life may not be smooth and perfect, God is merciful. Enmity toward clergy will remain. As the old saying puts it 'not until the sea dries up and the devil is taken up into heaven, will the layman be a true friend of the clergy.'"[2]

Now, on to some of my own parish remembrances, starting with my first year in ministry.

2. Luther, *Letters of Spiritual Counsel*, 304.

CHAPTER 11

St. Martin Lutheran Church, Annapolis, MD (1973–74)

SINCE WE HAD KNOWN each other only through three seasons, the fourth season (summer) was new to us. The apartment complex had a swimming pool and we tried it out. Judy was a proficient swimmer having been a lifeguard. I could barely dog paddle. She thought a sexy move would be to come up and under and grab me around the neck. I panicked and thought I would drown. We had some things to learn about each other, including schedules where she had to commute for course work in D.C. In some of the monasteries where classes were held, she was the only woman, the only one married, and the only Lutheran. They had to post a paper sign: "Ms. Cobb's restroom." It was a quick test of the Washington Theological Consortium's ecumenical hospitality.

My senior pastor decided that since I came onto staff, he would take a long overdue vacation. "Don't worry," he said, "the Danish exchange students will be here for a week. They have an itinerary and our bus driver will move you around," and off he went. We had two Danish teenage girls in our apartment for a week in our first month of marriage. They were a bit more visible in their night clothes than Americans might be used to. Their attire was a bit revealing and I admit to distraction (but nothing that would ever land me in trouble). One of the girls was named Bente. Years later, as I had shared this story with family members, my nephew became pastor of the international congregation in Copenhagen. One day, he and his wife passed a shop called "Bente's Lingerie," but alas, no connection for once. Also, the group of Danish teens were taken to a July 4th celebration and we all sat in the upper deck of the Naval Academy football stadium for the fireworks display. The problem was the wind was blowing and several fire balls ended up around us in the upper deck. No fires or injuries to report, but very close calls.

Our first Sunday at St. Martin, a lady with a distinct southern accent came up and asked "are you Ellen's boy?" "Guilty," I said. She told how her father was a pastor in SC and she had spent some summers in my grandparent's home with my Mom in Columbia, SC. Small world for "connections." She graced us with some delicious lemon meringue pies over the next year.

After a wonderful parish internship, I was raring to go. Judy and I had rounded up some cast-off furniture, we each had our books and a fellow student was ready to drive a U-Haul. The apartment was down the hill from the parish. Our bookcases were boards on bricks. Improvisation is the mother of invention when one has little money for furnishings.

—In Annapolis, I officiated at my first wedding: The bride was a theater major at the Univ. of MD, the groom was soon to be an engineering grad of the Naval Academy. In her conversation with me, she worried about the groom memorizing his vows and speaking them in public. He just wasn't used to a "stage" as she was. On the day of the wedding, the groom was flawless. On the other hand, her nerves got the best of her and she had to be fed her cues, word for word. Finally, we arrived at the pronouncement of marriage to the relief of all.

In Annapolis, I had my first funeral. Arriving home, Judy asked how did it go? I said that in my talk about heaven, if I had asked the congregation who wanted to go, now, yes now, they would have all raised their hands. I learned I must give a bit of deference to death and grief and maybe the gathering was not quite ready to storm the heavenly gates quite yet. Young preachers have a lot to learn.

—My first parish visit led to a near traumatized resolve to quit visiting. One of the active families invited me over. They had three small children. The oldest, Stephen, asked if I wished to see his pet. "Of course," I answered (thinking it would be a dog, cat, hamster, or goldfish?) He bounded down the steps with a hand behind his back, and viola-he had a pet snake. It was a scare-me-out-of-my clerical-collar moment. Today, Stephen serves as a Lutheran pastor and it was a privilege to assist in his parents' funeral years later. (Connections!) Live and learn.

—We had a young organist who was a grad student as our music director, she was super talented and energetic. She lived with an aunt while attending grad school. Judy and I were invited to their house and their German Shepherd came bounding out toward us with a stick in its mouth. I decided it wanted to play catch, grabbed the stick and the dog grabbed my upper arm, punctured the jacket, shredded the shirt underneath and I had to end up with a doctor's visit and have the scar to this day. Irony: The house had been broken into during the last week and the burglars had no attention from the "watchdog." It only attacked the pastor later. Moral: Approach people's pets with caution.

—When my parents first came to visit, my mother complained of a migraine headache. I told her I had a cure. I gave my tee-totaling mother a cordial of Drambuie, she gulped it down, felt the fire down her throat, took her breath away and she told others there was indeed a cure for migraines that "Jimmy" had in a dark bottle.

One of my first parish "mix-ups" came with what I thought was a dinner invitation at the church door as a family exited one Sunday. There was a family named Strohl who taught at the Naval Academy and had college-aged children and a family named Stoll who was a Naval commander with college-aged children. I called the Strohl's to thank them for the invitation to dinner, asking again about the date and time. They sheepishly said that if one or the other had extended the invitation, they forgot it. "No trouble," I said (and secretly thinking it would be good to have a free evening at home.) We had an early dinner and I went out to a car wash and began waxing the car. Judy frantically came with her car screeching to a halt with the news that the Stoll's had called and we were late for dinner. A mad dash later and we arrived for a "second dinner" for the evening! The result of this confusion of my making was that we agreed that Judy would be the keeper of the social calendar and that has worked for our lifetime.

That summer, as the secretary went on vacation, a recent college grad (named Strohl) came to cover the office while laughing at my faux pas. She was a German major and the number one graduate of Vassar. Fluent in German and being Lutheran, I said, "you must have read Luther in German." "No," she said. I challenged her to do so even as she was preparing to train as a paralegal. Two years later I heard she entered Gettysburg Seminary, then parish ministry, then a Phd in Reformation studies at the University of Chicago. She became a scholar in two of our seminaries and has remained a friend through the years.

Some months into the parish setting, tragedy struck when I received a Saturday morning phone call from parishioners that their thirteen- year-old son had hung himself in their home basement. The couple had become early friends in the parish and to this day, I see the scene as I drove them to the funeral home as they sat in the back seat of my VW shivering in each other's cold embrace. They would never know whether he was playing with an idea or was intentional in his act.

Within a year, I had become less than enthusiastic about the lack of relationship with the senior pastor. I soon learned that he had not wanted an Assistant Pastor and, in fact, had written two different job descriptions first, for a lay assistant, second, as a pastoral assistant and then the Council had arranged for a call to an Assistant Pastor. In his eyes, my main duty was to lock the church facility in the evenings. I was restless and put in a call to my home synod president with the request to be considered for a call back in Virginia. He had two parishes in mind and a call committee from Christ Lutheran Church, in Fredericksburg, Virginia set a time to come to an evening chapel service on Palm Sunday. I decided to read the Gospel from the center aisle, stepped out to do so but had forgotten both my bulletin with the text and I had not carried a Bible with me. I realized too late but I was not about to turn around and retrieve what I needed and be thus embarrassed, so I told the story from memory, having heard it in the morning worship. The call committee would later say how impressive and dramatic that had been and that was definitely a positive moment in the whole experience. Judy graduated from seminary with her M.A.R. degree and we were off to a new place and a new call.

Chapter 12

Christt Lutheran Church,
Fredericksburg, VA (1974–81)

THIS SLEEPY, SMALL COLLEGE town was about to explode into
a metro population. Federal government employees found the
D.C. environs too expensive for housing and this brought a
boom to Fredericksburg. Many parishioners would come with
backgrounds in all sorts of disciplines. Military and government
workers came from every region of the country. Many who were
Lutheran sought the church and we were the lone option for a
while between northern VA and Richmond. These young families wanted a church "home," and the church came to be a center-
piece of friendship and community building. We would be here
for seven years and maintain some close friendships through
all these years. Our synod President said, "you will always have
a special memory of your first real parish," and that is so true.
When we arrived the small numbers of parishioners scattered
through four exits in the church. Then came a church softball
league and suddenly this was the spark that ignited friendships.
One night, I counted 70 parishioners in the stands, including
small children. The church became an extended family for these

displaced federal workers! Noticeably on Sundays, people did not run to the exits but stayed and clogged the aisles, enjoying one another's visits. Fellowship group events reinforced relationships and the congregation grew in numbers. We began a new preschool that continues to flourish. Weddings and baptisms increased, campus ministry was significant. The synod provided an intern to survey surrounding areas with the possibility of a new mission congregation (and one would begin in Stafford County.) This intern did a fair job of survey work. Judy and I left on vacation and invited them to stay at our home. When we returned, we found the stove had to undergo a repair, a mantle clock quit working (probably to silence the Westminster chimes) and my tennis racquet was busted. The same intern had been visiting far out into the rural countryside when he ran out of gas, walked to a station a couple of miles back and left his wristwatch as collateral for $5 of gas. Yes, he did retrieve it later. Remember, these were the days *before* cell phones. Oh well, why would we remember such moments?

Judy had three jobs through this tenure. She was a teacher's assistant in high school reading; she taught religion at community college and then a job three days per week on a radio show called "Community Forum." (Some of the interviewees on the radio show included Joe Theismann, Frank Mankiewicz, an astronaut, and her first migraine headache with the Phyllis Schafly vs. NOW as each side came with an attorney to insure equal time.) One month when we were broadcasting services on her station, she was the lector. She mispronounced a word and declared, "O God, holy and immoral . . ." The letter "t" can make a difference. Upon returning to the station, someone had made a poster that read "Holy and immoral God." In her spare time, she served on a board to build a new "Y" and the opening of a pastoral counseling center. She was and always has been, a key catalyst for church fellowship and Christian Education and youth ministry events. Her partnership in ministry through the years has been such a significant part of any parish successes.

We hoped to begin a family during this time. But various tests told us that we each had problems and may not be able to conceive. We prepared adoption papers and had a specialist in Richmond to meet us one last time. He explained that for the final consult, he would again go over tests to tell us why we could not have children and he left the room for a final physical only to come back red-faced saying, "forget what I said, you're pregnant." Judy's parents, Margaret and Howard Dawson, came down immediately for a celebratory dinner. I insisted on paying and Howard finally said, "ok but I've got the drinks." "No, I've got this." Judy said, "look on the back." The bar bill was more than the food bill and I quickly thanked Howard for the offer. Back home, Judy threw up as Howard yelled "there goes her $50 tab down the toilet." He was humorous that way! Christopher James would be born on Nov. 18, 1976, a Bicentennial baby! He was truly the church's child and posters went up on the church steps and Judy's radio colleagues announced it on WFLS radio. We would be in Fredericksburg through his preschool years and some of the antics we learned about a child and church are appended to this manuscript in what I wrote entitled, "Laughing Through the Church with a Three-Year-Old."

In 1976, all Lutheran congregations received a special letter from our presiding national president that we were challenged to help resettle Vietnamese refugees. Without committees or council, I read the communique and had a hand-drawn piece of cardboard suggesting that we would have an offering procession (unusual for Lutherans) and people could sign in under the categories of: housing—clothing—food—transportation—money—or other. The response was immediate and overwhelming. Now the Council could vote to proceed with data to back it up! The first family of four arrived and would become a huge success story with their infants learning English and eventually becoming college grads and corporate stars. The father in this family called me one day frantic that his son had fallen off a tricycle and had a bloody cut. I got them to the ER and as the stitches were being inserted, the father was about to pass out (he had been a jet pilot in Vietnam but this personalized injury affected him mightily.) About a year into their new life, Judy and I took them to a bank to set up accounts for checking and savings. He went over to the manager and said, "tell me about CD's." The manager explained that when someone had accumulated $1000, a CD would be a good investment for saving. Then he said, "I'll take three." (I myself had accumulated none!)

The congregation decided in 1977 to sponsor a second family of four and in 2019, I was invited to the "baby's" swearing in as the only Vietnamese-American congresswoman in the U.S. House of Representatives, Stephanie Murphy (D-FL). Both sons in these families are now successful businessmen. Both girls in the two families are graduates of my alma mater, College of William and Mary, and we are so proud!

The 1977 resettlement family called me one day in a panic. Could I come over? I went and they said they had heard from a neighbor that their house had been the scene of a death and this explained why their Buddhist ancestor-spirits were displeased which they knew because the candles were dripping on the wrong side. I asked, "What do you want me to do?" They answered, "Bring the cross, pray to Jesus." The next day I was there with a confirmation cross, hammered it on the wall and prayed to Jesus. Afterwards, the candle dripped on the right side and all was well. I did not hang out a shingle advertising "exorcisms." (But this was my one and only.)

The congregation had three members of the FBI faculty from their Quantico academy. The largest adult forum ever was a session led by the agent who had been a chief interviewer with Charles Manson. Seems that murder draws a crowd. Wish I could say the same for Bible studies.

We always had the church councils at our home for a reception to start a new year. In Fredericksburg, it poured rain that night and the council president stepped into a deep rut and puddle of water. He came into the house asking if I could lend him some dry socks. Happy to oblige, I got them back the next Sunday, in the offering plate!

Judy had led a youth retreat at church, but being pregnant she could not sleep on the floor, for their all-nighter, so I was given the assignment to be an overnight monitor. I had the boys in one room and decided to sleep in the doorway to prevent any "escapes." (Please know that except for Christopher's birth night, I had never, ever pulled an all-nighter in my life!) I woke up early at about 6 AM to find 4 boys gone! The parsonage was next door and I ran over to Judy to admit the disappearance of 4 youth and ask what to do. She counseled, "Try the 7–11 at the end of the street. They have a new video game called "Pac Man." Yep, that's where I rounded up the four strays, brought them back into the fold and thus ended my less-than-successful chaperoning experience.

When Judy had a three day a week job taping radio interviews, I was a stay-at-home Dad with Christopher every Friday. We stayed in pajamas, played with Lincoln logs or legos, took naps on the living room rug and let dishes pile up in the kitchen.

Judy occasionally had to go out of town for some meetings. The first time she went away, I bought a portable dishwasher; the second time, an electric grill, all to enhance and conserve time for play!

One Sunday, I saw that our chalice was about to run out of wine and I needed a choir member to move to the sacristy for a refill. I pointed to the chalice and said, "More." He replied, "No thanks, I've already had some."

On my last Sunday in Fredericksburg, VA, I was at the point in the liturgy of "breaking the bread." I began the task when Judy said she noticed the tension in my forearms along with redness in my neck and she thought I was emotional about that last service, when suddenly the loaf went "pop" because it was frozen! It was before microwave ovens and the altar guild assumed it would thaw in 2 hours before it was needed. It didn't.

The parish affirmed my working on a grad degree beginning in 1977. I took summer course work at Gettysburg and Philadelphia's combined program with additional study at Catholic Univ. The degree of Doctor of Ministry was conferred in 1980 with a focus in "Worship, Preaching and Liturgics."

Part of my Doctor of Ministry project was the writing and use of "liturgical time capsules." One took place in our furnace rooms to represent "catacombs" worship. Persons entered with a password, someone brought candles, someone brought bread, someone brought wine. Then an elderly lady representing Mary stood to tell how she had been an eyewitness to Jesus and told her story. Children's eyes became huge with wonder and she would always be known as the woman who knew Jesus! This wonderful lady had been a teacher in Iowa and an aid to the NSA. Her name was Helmke but Christopher called her "Miz Hunky."

A German professor of religion at Mary Washington College asked if I would be involved in proposing a special monument commemorating Thomas Jefferson's writing of Virginia's Declaration of Religious Freedom in Fredericksburg. He gathered funding and the commemoration was accomplished with Lutheran, Catholic, Jewish and Muslim representatives taking part.

It is a church blessing to have good secretaries who can save you and others. I remember one day the secretary relayed a message that a person she had talked with did not sound right to her. I went over and found the woman contemplating suicide; the intervention worked and literally a life was saved. Thank you to the parish administrative assistants whose tasks involve much more than bulletins and newsletters!

The African American Mayor of Fredericksburg was pastor of Shiloh Baptist Church. As President of the area Ministerial Association, I was invited to have the invocation as his church celebrated its anniversary. I went up to pray. Just a couple of phrases in, I was joined by a piano, after a prayer phrase a couple of folks said "Amen," a few said "Say it again" so I did. Then an organ joined in. In my brain, I thought I would pray until the music signaled an end, but they kept going and so did I. In just a few moments, they trained me to be a rhythmic preacher, repeating phrases and listening for responses. After I figured the musicians were waiting for me to get to an Amen, I finally concluded after one of the longest prayers in my history! When I sat down, Judy said "You enjoyed yourself, didn't you?" Yes, I did.

1976 was the nation's Bicentennial year. On July 4, we invited the congregation to dress in colonial garb if available and we would use the well-known colonial Lutheran liturgy of the church's American patriarch, Henry Melchior Muhlenberg. It was a festive, memorable day.

Nelly McCauley taught me the importance of wearing a clerical collar. Her daughter invited me to sit with her Mom who was eighty-nine years old as she was in and out of a coma. One time she woke up and saw me and said, "Thank you Pastor for confirming me." (I had not.) Another time she awakened to say, "Thank you Pastor for marrying us." (I had not.) Another time, she said, "Thank you Pastor for burying my parents." (I had not.) All of this meant that the clerical collar she saw in the corner, represented important times in her life when a pastor had been present. What a gift for someone to have it connected to special moments through her life. This was a blessing!

One Sunday, Judy asked after church, if I had been distracted during my sermon. "About what?" I asked. A child vomited in the right front pew and ushers came in with bucket and mop. "No," I said, "never saw them." Preaching must occur "in the zone."

I remember the only acolyte to stand in front of the church and watch his "rope cincture" unravel around his waist and hit the ground. He was an eagle scout. Aren't they supposed to know how to tie knots?

One wedding I will remember because it was the only time that I saw a groomsman faint over all these years. While the couple knelt, I whispered that a groomsman had keeled over and we would take him out so stay kneeling until I returned. His uncle and I carried him out. When he came to, he saw me dressed in white and his uncle (I kid you not) was an undertaker. He nearly passed out again from fright!

I learned in Fredericksburg to leave the church organist in charge of music. A couple asked if their cousin who was a child prodigy in organ could accompany the wedding because he played the largest pipe organ in northern Virginia. "Yes," I said, "that will be a treat." I learned too late that the largest pipe organ in northern Virginia was not in a church, but in a skating rink. The processional was the hit song, "Turn Around Look at Me." (Never again!)

During an annual meeting, we had a new member nominated for Council. One of the tenured members began to speak about the fact that newcomers should have tenure before nomination. I called his remarks "out of order," to the gasp of the whole assembly. But sometimes the hammer of Robert's Rules must be the guide. (So too, the church's constitution.)

One member told me that she would always remember my green VW super beetle. I asked why. She said that in funeral processions, she saw these long, black limos with caskets and family in procession and then the small green bubble of a car. She said it was like a sprig of new life chasing death. You never know what symbols people see!

Fredericksburg nearly cured me of ever doing a "children's' sermon." I had a good baptismal talk about water. Water helps things grow. Water goes into plants and fruits. And water does one more thing, let me see if you can answer this question: "You've been outside on a hot Saturday and you've been playing, you come in on Saturday night and you're very dirty, what happens?" One little girl spoke out, "Mommy and Daddy take showers together." My back was to the congregation; the laugh broke into a cavernous explosion. The parents sat right behind me in the front pew, I could imagine their red faces. I was shaking like an earthquake had hit my body. After what seemed an interminable length of time, the laughter quieted and then the little girl said, "and then Mommy and Daddy lock the bathroom door and giggle a lot." Laughter, with eruption number two. I was almost cured. I met the child who grew into a young adult some 25 years later. She had no memory of such an event. God is good.

During these years, our Cobb family often rented a large beach house on the Outer Banks of NC. The largest summer church attendance was the Sunday after our vacation in order to hear what "disaster" happened this year. We had several in a row. One summer, our eldest had a splinter from a deck that took a doctor to remove. When he started to do this, the child's pain reacted with a swift kick into the doctor's groin. Since he was a new resident, he learned how to protect himself. The prescription we filled was expensive and we got there just before the pharmacy closed. I went out, they locked the door and I proceeded to drop the bottle and smash the contents. They saw what happened, re-opened and charged half price for the second bottle. We went to the outdoor drama, "Lost Colony," with a three-year old niece who had two uncles and two Lutheran pastor grandfathers. In the opening scene, the first new colony baptism of Virginia Dare was portrayed. The minister said, "I baptize thee, Virginia Dare in the Name of the Father and of the Son and of the Holy Ghost." At which point the niece in her tiny soprano voice sang, "Amen!" The people around us laughed, the players on stage did not know what had happened but had to pause to re-capture the audience. One year, our nephew (age 7), threw up just after climbing out of the car in the parking lot. To allay the smell, we sprayed him with mosquito spray and went in. Another year, we were all evacuated because we were in the path of a hurricane. Another year, an oil spill dotted the beach with nuggets of oil all around. Another year, a waterspout turned into a tornado and hit land killing one and doing a million dollars in damage. At our departure party by the church, they presented us with a document purportedly from the Outer Banks Chamber of Commerce, noting our family disasters and commending us to our new environs in Michigan! The send-off "roast" was good. The vacation experiences brought the family together with good food, good stories and relative bonding for the extended group with occasional arguments over "Rook," and other latent squabbles. Good times.

CHAPTER 13

Trinity Lutheran Church, Grand Rapids, MI (1981–88)

THERE IS ONE JUNE Friday in 1980 in Fredericksburg that I will never forget. In the mail, I had a packet of materials from our Bishop to consider a call to another church in Virginia. While reading the packet, I received a phone call from the SC Bishop about a church he wished me to consider in West Columbia. After I hung up, I had a call from the Michigan Bishop about a church in East Grand Rapids. I called my Bishop and asked what I should do. I said, "I am getting a hint that I should consider a new call." He said, "visit them all and see what you think." I did. I learned later that the Virginia Bishop was initiating the church in VA, a SC cousin had put my name forward in SC, and a former parishioner from Fredericksburg had put forward my name when their pastor had recently been elected Bishop. Of course, take the most difficult one, the most challenging one, uproot your family and go where no Cobb had gone before. I had never been in Michigan and thought it must be out there next to Montana or something (I admit I had to look at a map to get the geography located.) Oh, how youth venture bravely into the unknown!

So, how did the Grand Rapids call come about? One of our Fredericksburg members was a child psychiatrist. He finished his military commitment and opened a private practice in our town. After about 4 years, he received a call to consider relocating back to his home turf in Michigan. The only church-sponsored, residential, pediatric psychiatric hospital was close to Grand Rapids and he had returned close to his home. When his pastor was elected Bishop, he submitted my name and the call committee interviewed and we were off to a new adventure. Trinity was one of the largest congregations in the Lutheran orbit both in membership (1800) and financial resources. The departing pastor was 58, I was coming in at 33. It would be a challenge. It was also in a three-pronged religious environment: Dutch Reformed, Polish Catholic and German/Scandinavian Lutherans. When I went out to choose a house, almost nothing was on the market. A church member/realtor took me on a night visit to a small cottage type of home, but the electricity was off and I saw it when he lit a match in the dark night. A local police car pulled up behind us in the driveway wondering who we were and what we were doing. This small town of East Grand Rapids was its own municipality and they paid attention to any strange goings-on. This was a year when mortgages topped 14%; this one was assumable at 11% and such a deal! Judy said "Tell me what you saw, did it have an oven?" "I think so. I remember the thick carpet in the house and some kind of jungle wallpaper in one bedroom." That was it. A congregational loan provided for a down payment and so we went. What no one told me was that two cars needed a two-car garage for brutal winters. One stayed on the street and the snowplow would encase it every wintery day. We found a wonderful preschool at Temple Emanuel for Christopher and it would be four blocks from his elementary school. Judy quickly made an OB/GYN appointment as we again considered adoption. At her first appointment, the doctor looked over her case and said, "You really gave birth with all these tests against you?" A physical was performed and he came in to say, "Child number two is on the way." We had astonished doctors twice! Stephen would be born on Oct. 30, 1981. His birth was early and Christopher had just gone in for ear tubes surgery when Judy's water broke and she wanted to avoid a "Reformation" baby on Oct. 31 to avoid the names Martin or Luther or Melancthon. A plea for help to Judy's mother was made and after her evening dinner party, she caught a plane and came to us in our hour of need. In the meantime, the good friend's family formerly from Fredericksburg took Christopher and we have been forever grateful. They became Stephen's godparents at baptism.

This church was a wonderful twenty-acre campus with modern Byzantine architecture (an impressive circular sky dome over a round, marble chancel), quite unique, but splendorous in musical and organ reverberation. An entire choir had left another church and ventured over to Trinity a year or so before and I would have to deal with those dynamics for some time. This would be the largest choir in any of our parishes and the director and organist are memorable for their talent and dedication in our staff working together. The long- time secretary helped me with hints such as "The last pastor sent a postcard to every member on their birthday, you don't want to do that do you?" One task eliminated.

The first Sunday I was there, a woman came up and referred to my bio and said, "I see you went to William and Mary. Did you know my brother, he taught religion, his name is James Livingston?" I replied that "he had been super-influential in my going to seminary and becoming a pastor." She noted that he came to West Michigan to a cottage every summer and he would want to get together. We did and it was a good friendship over the years. When Livingston's mother, who was a nursing home resident, died, they asked me to officiate at the funeral. Her pastor had moved away and the chaplain had retired, so 14 years after sitting in Livingston's classroom in Williamsburg, Virginia, I was officiating at his mother's funeral in Grand Rapids, MI. (Connections are strange, mysterious, and wondrous).

On my first Sunday at Trinity, I began a chanted liturgy and all heads in the pews snapped up. I would learn immediately that they had never heard a chanted liturgy though the hymnal included all the notes for such matters. That, along with the weekly Eucharist, were new things for Trinity.

Approaching 100 years old, Mabel Johnson took it upon herself to hand stitch a cross into every baptism napkin as a gift from the church.

Hulda and Leon Johnson were a retired couple whose presence was a gift before every worship, funeral, etc. to be true "doorkeepers in the house of the Lord," seeing that all things were in order.

Tillie Gallmeyer was a 96-year-old matriarch who attended church every week. After a new sound system had been installed, she came through the line and declared, "Pastor, that was the first sermon I've heard in 25 years!" Nice to know.

Another time, we had a youth event with the teens presenting a chancel drama that began with a classroom out of control. It was good drama, but I got a letter that week from Tillie. She objected to having seen a paper airplane fly across the altar.

I was informed by a parishioner that the church had six millionaires who, he was certain, were responsible for the financial viability of the church. The leading giver was a retiree! It reminded me of a similar fact in the Fredericksburg parish with all those well-paid federal workers. The leading giver was a retired teacher. The widow's mites still impact the church.

Some congregations have "tribal chiefs," those whose longevity and tenure give them a power that can sometimes become oppositional to a new pastor and new ideas. We had one such person at Trinity Church. He had been elected to the church council every time he was eligible since WWII! A kind way of putting it would be that he was a stumbling block to new ideas. Anyway, at the conclusion of his sixth year during my tenure, I honored him at the annual meeting with gifts thanking him for his continuous service to the congregation over many years. We had a wonderfully framed picture of the church presented and a long-stemmed rose saying, "This bud's for you," and everyone understood this was a "retirement from service" moment. Now in his late eighties, he too got the message.

Because I came in at such a young and inexperienced age, one of my best staff moves was to call a semi-retired pastor to join the staff. He was trusted (by age) where I might not be; he had wisdom and shared it with me often in a mentoring way and we so enjoyed him, his wife (she remained a lifelong friend after his early death following heart surgery); and I share two of his favorite stories. He said he often went to sit at the train station in order to see something move that he did not have to push! Second, he had served a church in New Haven, Connecticut and had several Yale Divinity professors in his congregation. One day a professor came through the line and said, "That was one of the best sermons I've ever heard on that text." Five minutes later, another came through and whispered, "What the hell did that have to do with anything?" He said that it taught me that the listener has much to do with preaching. So true! This great friend died too early in his retirement. It was quite sudden after carotid artery surgery and his extended family and the congregation grieved. A large funeral was held with many colleagues from the Lutheran School of Theology in Chicago attending where he had served in Stewardship and Development.

This congregation too was challenged to help resettle refugees, this time Ethiopians. When they arrived, an apartment had been prepared and the woman in charge greeted them one Saturday night. As she was about to leave, she said, "Pastor, I did work here all day; I'm tired so I think I'll skip church tomorrow." The Ethiopian spoke up, "In our country when we are tired, we miss work, not church." Delighted pastors beamed and would always remember. As they came to be enfolded by the congregation, we noticed some things. When the baby was baptized, they had not revealed the baby's name. In their Orthodox tradition, they whispered the name to the priest who then announced it (what a good custom!) Also, before we Lutherans had even caught on to younger age communions, the Ethiopians communed infants. I gave the wafer to the mother and she gave a small piece to the child. I would not excommunicate a baby and we learned a new thing.

The second Ethiopian family we sponsored had three daughters in their twenties. One had to have minor surgery. The next evening, they called me with the plea that I had to come and see the red streak at the surgery site. I asked what the surgery was called and they said it was for a "tipped uterus." I had no idea what this site might be and I did not want to go by myself. Judy was at some event and not available. The nurse in the congregation was not available either, so I sheepishly went to the home. They greeted me with "You need to see this." I have ever been naïve about female anatomy and surgeries but was relieved to find that it was across a belt line, via the belly button. I had pictured something that would yield much more blush-causing embarrassment. I finally got hold of her doctor who prescribed extra strength Tylenol and healing commenced.

One of the wealthy couples in the parish asked if we could get our best babysitter for a lengthy evening dinner. We did and as a surprise they took us to the airport to board their four-seater plane and flew us down the coast of Lake Michigan for dinner in Chicago! That was a journey we will always remember.

One of the finest ecumenical agencies we ever worked with was called "GRACE," Grand Rapids Area Center for Ecumenism. In this Dutch Reformed community, at the time, they sponsored one of the largest hunger walks in the nation. About 120 churches were active participants. In January, as a six-week ecumenical project, churches were selected to have the pastor give a lecture in the tradition's theology of the Eucharist followed by the worship service in that tradition and where permitted, to invite worshippers to commune. Trinity had a huge write-up in the local paper about such hosting. I served as board President, and I remember signing a bank loan for $40,000 as a bridge loan for cash flow purposes. I gulped and thought this was a huge "out on a limb" moment having never signed such an amount except for house mortgages! GRACE also sponsored a "Peace Links" service and communities around the nation quilted pieces for a gigantic "ribbon" to emphasize hope for peace. We hosted Betty Bumpers in our home for a small group meeting. She was the wife of Sen. Dale Bumpers of Arkansas and in that conversation, she predicted that their Governor, Bill Clinton, would one day be President and that was prophetic.

One of my wedding memories is about a couple who went through the pastoral conversations and planning and in the last session, they admitted to having been married a year before and had kept it secret from their families. When they asked me to do the same, I said that we could not have their marriage beginning with a lie, so in a change of direction, I insisted that they tell their families, and the service would proceed as a celebration of "re-affirming their vows." This service would begin with an announcement that they had been legally married on such-and-such a date. They agreed, their parents were ok with the news and the service was a celebration. (I would later get the same request in Norfolk, Virginia from a Naval officer, I said the same thing, but he and the bride refused and went out of state to another clergy who would keep their secret!) All such matters do not always end well.

One Sunday, I arrived at church and there was a wonderful spray of white flowers in the altar vase. In the middle of the white flowers, there was one red flower and it looked so out of place that I decided it was a mistake, so I took it out. Later the donor chastised the florist saying that for years that one red flower was a symbol for her dead husband. I admitted my fault and would seldom ever again, have commentary about church flowers.

One year, for Wednesday worship services in Lent, a new member of the altar guild wanted one arrangement in the vase that would represent "death," through the Wednesdays. At one point, it resembled some sort of driftwood with briars and brambles. It was hideous but I had nothing to say about it!

One more altar guild reference. One lady dedicated her flowers each year but always wanted the Hawaiian red petal flower with a single protruding red stem. When first seen, our son called them "little boy flowers" and I can never see them without thinking how he labeled them well!

Pastors at Trinity usually wore a one-piece white robe called an alb. But for Lent, with a different emphasis and mood, we wore a traditional cassock and surplice. I went out and turned back to the congregation and had the white surplice gathered up around my neck. Some would say that it reminded them of Batman, for reasons unknown.

One summer day, Christopher ran through the house, aimed for the front door, and missed, hitting the latch and his arm went through the glass door. Trip to the ER for stitches happened next with his tears and pain being obvious. It's a parent's suffering to see the child in pain. However, the attending doc rolled up his sleeve to reveal an almost identical scar when a similar childhood accident happened to him. They became friends for the duration of 30+ stitches.

Acolytes are an interesting bunch of teens who either love to serve or do so begrudgingly. One Sunday, an acolyte was running late and dashed into the sacristy, threw on a robe. She lit the candle-lighter and thinking I would be helpful, I reached out for the lit match as she opened the door to the sanctuary. She proceeded to drop the lit match into the palm of my hand. My muffled inappropriate words were never heard, simply thought!

I often served as 'Christopher and friends' transport to pre-school. In my small VW Beetle, I would throw junk mail in the back seat floor along with candy and ice cream wrappers and clean it all out every couple of months. One morning, I pulled the seat forward for the friend to get in the back; he looked and said, "I won't step in that mess." I took a snow scraper, laid it on top of the mess and said, "here's a bridge and you can walk across it." That was agreeable, problem solved.

One Sunday a woman came through the-after-church and said she was new to the area and would be joining our church. I asked how she could decide after one Sunday. She said she always had a "sign" when going to a new location. "What was your sign here?" I asked. She said, "I pulled into your parking lot and my radiator exploded." (And the people of Israel were led by a pillar of fire by night and a pillar of cloud by day!)

One sermon I preached and used a line saying, "Grace is the one sustaining note through all the Scriptures." And this was a repeated phrase through the sermon. At the end of the last hymn, an organ cipher stuck, and one note continued for the duration of time. Many thought it was a planned illustration. It was not planned!

A couple in the church adopted a boy from Brazil. On his first Sunday, his hands rested quietly on the balcony rail. He had secretly torn a bulletin into small pieces. During the sermon he pushed it all down in a rain of confetti. Only the back pew people and me, from the pulpit, could see the cloud descending from on high.

One of my real delights in parish ministry is gathering a small group of clergy, usually 6–8, ostensibly to discuss next Sunday's texts, but more as a sharing time among the group. One week I had seen someone bring in some "junk for Jesus," a box of stuff from an attic; it included a whiskey flask but the real "find" was a trophy that featured the rear end of a horse (I'm not kidding). I knew that the Pope often named a secret Cardinal of the church "in curia" (i.e., in the heart,) someone whose name and title had to be kept secret. I proposed, at each clergy meeting, that some pastor would grab the trophy and offer a story about some parishioner who ought to be an "in curia" recipient of the "rear end of a horse award." The resulting laughter was a very necessary in-house therapy for the clergy!

One pastoral act for which I was never prepared was with a young couple across the street that were members of our church. One morning while the dad was at work, the mom came screaming across the street that the youngest daughter somehow had sliced off a toe under a door frame and could I take them to the ER. Of course, I had to calm the girls and get them to the ER. The doctor came out and asked if I could go back to the house, retrieve the severed toe, put it on ice and get it back ASAP. I did. The toe was saved but that was one moment with no preparation for the mission of hunting for a severed toe. Wow. Pastors can all tell their own stories.

I will never forget one particular funeral in Grand Rapids. A lady called from Arizona and her son, in his forties, had died in Florida and their last family church had been Trinity, so could we have the funeral? Of course. I would meet her at the funeral home on the night of visitation. She was this petite, silver-haired Mom who was so proud of her son with glowing memories of his life, though geography had separated them over these past years. After a delightful conversation, she said, "I will go and bring his wife in and you two can talk." What came next was a pastor's nightmare: the "wife" appeared, and if ever one used the phrase "a lady of questionable appearance," she was it. She would best be described as a straggly, hair-twisting blond with loud gum-crackling pops dressed in a tight tiger-skin dress. (Oh, mother of the deceased, please don't leave me, but she did). Now we're on a couch in a side chapel. Her story went like this: "We hadn't been married long. We met in a bar and got married right away. I was his fifth wife. I don't know much about his spiritual life but the day he died, we walked along the beach and he said, 'isn't that sunrise beautiful?' so I guess that's kinda spiritual right? Anyway, we got back, had some fun if you know what I mean; he was taking a shower, collapsed and died. Now his first and third wife will be here tomorrow. But I do know that the third wife shot him. He has a bullet scar on his left shoulder, but his mother doesn't know that. She'll have him dressed in a shirt and tie but I saw to it that they put his favorite tee shirt on him with his favorite saying, "sh-—happens!" Hope this information helps." If ever there was a time to preach about a Mother's love for her son as she saw him, this was it. I couldn't help but glance at the body in the casket to at least see if the tee shirt could be seen. Thankfully, it could not!

This reminded me of my nephew's wife's funeral story. She grew up a Baptist in NC and told me about her youth pastor's story. A family's grandad had died and as was the custom, the visitation, with an open casket, was in the farmhouse some twenty miles outside the city and the pastor had been there in the evening. Later that night, they called this pastor and told him they needed him to come back, please come back, we'll tell you why when you get here. With his return trip, he found that they had never seen their grandad in a suit and tie and took him out of the casket, put him on a chair, and taped open his eyes in order to get a family picture! Now they could not get the body back in the casket and they were sure only a pastor would know how. Hence, the frantic phone call. True story!

Another pastor friend volunteered his true funeral story. It seems that pallbearers were called forward to prepare the casket for exit to the hearse and when the funeral director pulled down the lid and you heard it hermetically sealed with a "whoosh" sound, one pall bearer's necktie was caught in the lid. They had to pause, find scissors and cut his tie.

During these years, Judy worked part-time for GRACE in a hunger alleviation program. It was just the right balance between babies and work. After having two staff members in youth and Christian Education, the Council President came to me and said, "I know you are reluctant to have Judy on staff, but she is the most qualified and available person. Please don't object if we approach her with this offer." So, in 1986, we came together on the staff of Trinity. She worked wonders with both areas of ministry. I remember in confirmation class, I asked her to come in and teach a sexuality class to young teens. I just blushed too much and carried shyness with me, even after two children! I heard her begin the class saying, "We'll be using actual terms like intercourse, penis, testicles and not slang like screw, dick and nuts. I left turning red and knew they had a good and competent teacher. God gives differing gifts to different folks.

Do you know how they say, if you find a TV camera crew in your yard, it might be a bad sign? Well, that happened to me one Ash Wednesday. We found that a federal subpoena was issued with regard to our house's history and another in Florida. It seemed that the previous owner had falsified a federal F.H.A. loan and was charged with different counts of felonies. I testified that the closing sale had gone through, there was only one outstanding bill from a landscape company, otherwise all was free and clear and nothing else was asked of me and the house was not an issue. I was relieved.

There is always someone in every parish who is at least slightly mentally tilted. One such lady in Grand Rapids took over stitching the baptismal cross but she came in to see me all upset one day. She had received a package of "something" from Central America and upon opening it, some dust had come out. She was sure it was some kind of anthrax dust, and she could not do baptismal napkins if they might infect babies. I assured her that this was not a worry, and I would see to it that the napkins were disinfected and things went ahead as usual.

Trinity (Judy really) gave me a surprise fortieth birthday party. Unbeknownst to me, the organist postlude played bells for "Happy Birthday" and I was called back to the front to announce a special reception. My parents and one sister secretly came in, and southern foods were brought in: peanut butter crackers, Yoohoo soft drinks, boiled peanuts, spam, BBQ, etc. It was a great day. All of a sudden, the Ethiopians were loudly chattering around the boiled peanuts, it reminded them of something in their home country and they loved the treat. I was honored with a "this is your life" poster board and a shirt that read: "I'm from NC, VA, SC, TN, Japan, PA, MD, MI and my favorite phrase, "What difference does it make in the kingdom?" Great day, great memory.

In 1987, three national Lutheran church bodies merged to form the Evangelical Lutheran Church in America. National nominations were announced, and Judy was elected to the Division for Ministry and I was elected to the national Church Council. These meetings would dominate our lives over the next few years. It was an honor, but it was much work. She would serve until 1992 and I would serve until 1995.

In the gathering in Columbus, Ohio, I met the VA Synod Bishop and did not know that he would later be in touch with me about a call back to Virginia. A new chapter would begin.

CHAPTER 14

First Lutheran Church, Norfolk, VA (1988–99)

JUDY FOREVER JOKES THAT the Holy Spirit called me with a southern accent to come back east. I really do believe that there were four considerations: First, can weather really be part of a consideration? I am embarrassed to admit it but the weather was brutal, at least to me. I did have trouble adapting to winter clothing, heavy drapes pulled close all the time and gray skies nearly 80% of the time. I did not like winter sports and snow-plowing every morning due to "lake effect" snow showers. I did not do well with cross country skiing and ice skating. I did not adapt well to ice fishing, ice sailing, icicles from roof gutters and chopping ice around gutters. The length of winter was October through April. Not fun! As I look back, I think I did have "seasonal affective disorder" and today that recognized problem uses day lights for some relief. Second, the call to First Lutheran was a call into an urban ministry. Challenges seem to be directed at a more rag tag populace than wealthy suburbia. Third, the children were in school in East Grand Rapids where one black child was enrolled. That was to be an unreal orbit, or so we thought.

The fourth consideration was that Trinity was ready for a pipe organ replacement and a new building addition to expand its ballooning membership. I did not wish to lead a building project and wished that another pastor with such talents would be their next find. So, I was agreeable to the call. We left on Judy's fortieth birthday and her tears flowed all the way to Norfolk. No departure and "goodbyes" were ever to her liking. The arrival in Norfolk was to a brilliant sunny sky and the annual Azalea Festival. It was refreshing too as I felt like an energy source had been plugged in. The boys thought they might never see snow again, but the very next winter, Norfolk received a 12-inch, unexpected "snow-mageddon" and our sons were the only kids on the block with appropriate snow clothing-boots, hats, gloves, and heavy coats. They were thrilled! The boys were now going to be in classes about evenly divided with black and white students. Diversity would be a gift and a puzzle.

As I had followed a newly-elected Bishop in Michigan, I now followed a renowned preacher who had been the Lutheran radio preacher on the national "Protestant Hour." I had one advantage, as this pastor had been both a college and seminary classmate of my father. Thus, the two families had known each other for some time. First Lutheran, in addition to being the mother church of other missions in Tidewater, was a leading congregation in Virginia. They had a forty- year tenured pastor followed by a 20-year pastorate. The large gothic building, however, was in sad shape. Many parishioners only came into the sanctuary and that had remained in fairly good shape, but the rest of the building included original low seated toilets, rusted stalls, ceiling and wall leaks, etc., all needing attention and repair. When Judy's parents came for their first visit, a fellowship meal on the third floor, they saw some ceiling plaster fall onto her plate. Someone said, "Oh that's good; it means the plaster has dried out."

That very next winter, the furnace blew up and we had no heat. A flatbed truck came in as this Navy town was used to having to power large ships with similar needs. We made it through the winter. Now the church council was motivated to lead us into a major building renovation. I did not want to do "building" in Grand Rapids where there was ample money and a desire to expand, so why would I want to do this in Norfolk with less people, less means and less motivation? I felt like Jonah who ran away from the call and got spit up in Nineveh (Norfolk?) to do what he was called to do in the first place! Doesn't God have a sense of humor? First, there would be an engineering needs assessment, then a long-range plan, then an architect's hiring and drawings, followed by a congregational decision to proceed, then the hiring of a fund-raising firm. Disregarding the money for the first three phases, in 1990, the price tag looked like $1.4 million and it seemed to be a staggering goal. One long-tenured member made a plea for modern toilets and that argument seemed to rally the troops.

Judy came to Norfolk without a position. The Bishop had agreed that she should be considered as a staff associate and this "single" call became a major issue in our marriage. I had truly made an assumption that as senior pastor, I would be able to pick my staff, but this congregation was used to two pastors and this optional configuration was not without push-back. I proposed one or two retired pastors for visitation and Judy as full-time Director of Youth, Christian Education and Campus Ministry (ODU students had long been neglected). The council ultimately agreed to the position with probationary trial periods reviewed annually. One member quit over this supposed nepotism, but most suspiciously gave it a chance. Judy would remain embarrassed by the whole issue and to this day thinks it should have been negotiated first and not after, even if the call would have been withdrawn. In hindsight, she was right. This should have been shared up front to propose a team rather than afterwards with the pressure of leverage. The Bishop realized the controversy but affirmed the new staff design. With her good and competent work, the Sunday School grew, including adult course offerings, the youth group experienced its historical high point, and the campus ministry was not very successful with undergrads but was with grad students and young Navy types. They kind of found each other, came to our house every other Sunday night, and included four marriages through those years! The Church was located in a hospital-restaurant-theater area called "Ghent." The area pastors got together with each church, taking a day to feed the homeless (Lunch ministry) and each taking a week throughout the winter to house the homeless NEST (Norfolk Emergency Shelter Task). This was the 1990's and the programs still are viable today.

Pastors sometimes are asked to do funerals for anonymous persons. It usually begins with the funeral director calling and saying, "they were baptized Lutheran," and you know it will be a request. In one case, it was a grandmother from Tennessee whose unchurched grandson was killed in an auto wreck at age 19. I did the funeral and the family was appreciative. About a year later, I received a kind note from the grandmother and tickets to the Master's Golf tournament in Augusta, Georgia. What an unexpected surprise and a dream moment for this golf hacker who annually watches this gala on TV. I'll never forget the generosity!

One controversial prayer petition happened after a mass shooting and the NRA flexed its political power to defeat attempts at gun control, so I prayed for the demise of the NRA. It took 28 years to see the organization go bankrupt; sometimes prayers take a long time.

During one funeral, an elderly man sitting in the family pew said he was not sad during the service because Alice was present. I asked how he knew this. He said, during the whole service, a Chrismon (tree decoration) she had made for the large Christmas tree in front of him, twirled! It may have been a heating vent, but the sign was quite enough for him.

The Norfolk parish had quite a contingent of political folks: the mayor, Speaker of the House of Delegates, first woman President of the VA Bar Assoc., judges and various other attorneys. I was twice asked to open the General Assembly with prayer in Richmond. Once, Stephen went with me asking, "Who are those kids who are working?" This was his fifth-grade year, so in 7th grade he applied and went to Richmond for six weeks, thus beginning his interest in politics. At the conclusion of his session, I asked what was the difference between the two political parties? He said, "Democrats tip better." It seems to have made a lifelong impression!

In a Navy town like Norfolk, it was interesting to hear some young enlisted kid from the Midwest meet Admiral so-and-so in coffee hour. They were stunned when we would introduce one to the other on an equal footing because the church was such an equal community. Admirals were always gracious in such moments. The Naval officers often called on us for retirement or change of command ceremonies. It was a precise liturgy of transition to observe and serve. Early in my tenure, I asked some of our officers whether they expected special mention during Sundays around military dates (Memorial Day, 4th of July, Veterans Day). Universally, they said "no" and expected the church to follow its own protocols. They would comment that if they wanted such moments, they would be at the base chapel and not in a civilian parish. I was grateful too that the flags were in the narthex around a memorial plaque and not in the sanctuary. We Lutherans had learned from Germany that the flag ought not be with the cross!

One of my favorite stories at First Lutheran was this one: A lady in our church provided a month's housing for foreign students to reorient before graduate studies began. One such hostess housed a Chinese student who would earn a PhD in microbiology. She came to church and she stayed for the next five years! She was the daughter of a physician/Mom and an engineer/Dad. She said she came from northern China where no Christian missionary had ever ventured. She absorbed everything: Bible studies, worship, joined choir, and the young adult/campus group. She asked to be baptized; she was chosen as a delegate to the synod assembly. She became engaged to a grad student in our group who had a part-time job as our wedding coordinator who heard me lament that no one had ever chosen to get married during a Sunday worship. They came to talk to me about a Sunday morning wedding. She wore traditional Chinese formal dress. The liturgy had never seen a Sunday morning wedding. The congregation gave the "poor grad students" their reception in the fellowship hall with a wonderful brunch. With the help of a U.S. Senator, we were able to have her parents come for this festivity. The church was at its best in enfolding this couple in its embrace. I asked her afterwards why she kept coming back to church when it was so foreign to her. I expected to hear about the beauty of the stained glass, the wonders of the music, or maybe even the excellent preaching. She named a mentally challenged person whom she saw in that very first coffee hour. She said, "In my country we would have put him away; you all treated him like family. I wanted to know why." What a witness to the whole congregation. Today, she and her husband are parents of two children and both are in leading research vocations in Silicon Valley, California!

We had a parishioner named Ole Olsen. Most every Lutheran congregation in the USA probably has an Olsen debating whether they are Norwegian or Swedish. This Olsen was in his eighties when he stopped by to show me his new car. He insisted that I ride with him as the first passenger because over the years, the pastor had done this, and he was sure it was important. I went with Ole and concluded by asking, "Ole, what does a pastor's butt have to do with blessing your new car?" No answer. This same guy went out the front door one morning, saw a motorcycle parked out front and asked, "are bikers with leather and chains coming to church?" I said, "All are welcome." He said, "Good. The bike is mine!" Another time he was late for serving as an overnight monitor for our homeless shelter, he ran into the dark hall, tripped over a resident, broke his leg and the ambulance woke the entire group of guests as medics wheeled him out. Visiting the hospital, I accused him of using this as a sly way of getting out of his week's commitment.

Speaking of the homeless week in our church building, Judy was an overnight monitor and heard a ruckus in the women's restroom. She went in to check things out and found two enormous naked women in a sumo wrestling match, while slinging wet paper towels at each other. A much smaller Pastor Judy stepped between them, pushing them apart to later describe the "slow motion recall of the moment," in which she had one breast in her left hand and one in her right, thinking, "What the hell am I doing?" Blessed are the peacemakers!

The homeless ministry served by various close neighborhood churches had one episode I recall when I was doing an overnight monitoring stay. A sheriff came to the door with a warrant. He said that he had been told that a guest in our program had an outstanding warrant and they would come in to arrest him. It was around 11 PM and they turned on lights going from mat to mat to find one person; found him; got him up and out in handcuffs. I was disturbed by this action, waited a couple of weeks and went to have a chat with the sheriff. In replaying the episode in my mind, I asked what would you have done had I denied you entry? He said, "Arrested you for obstruction." "But I thought churches were understood to be a sanctuary for safe harbor." "Doesn't apply here," he said. In retrospect, as the country tries to grapple with the "Black Lives Matter" movement (2020 and forward), I certainly was timid in protecting a guest and I realize how witnesses standing by in the George Floyd killing must have felt really being helpless to intervene. We, as "church," must consider what it means to be a sanctuary and raise the question about where law enforcement might remain outside our doors.

—I had a part-time pastor assistant and he and I shared a communion set when we went to nursing homes. I scooped it up one day, went to visit a blind elder, set out the elements, only to find out that the wine bottle only had purple stains while I thought it had some wine in it, but it was empty. Since the woman was blind, I crept over to the faucet, poured some water in the bottle and swished it around. It was a miracle: water became wine. Neither she nor I ever told, but I did learn never to assume the communion set was ready to go without checking.

I was so honored to be an ELCA delegate to the Lutheran World Federation in Hong Kong in 1997. It was the first international assembly after Hong Kong's revision to mainland China. It caused nervousness about our reception, but all went well. Our hotels meant a ferry ride across from the convention hall each day. In one of the ferry's signs, the English meant to say "No solicitations allowed," but instead read "No sermons allowed!" This was quite a prohibition to the hundreds of pastors being ferried each day. I remember these things about the Assembly: first, the earphones. 1000 delegates from across all continents meant that translations could be dialed in via English, Spanish, French and German. At day's end, the inside of one's ear hurt. Second, the debate over a human rights resolution had the Chinese Lutherans asking for a temporary stay till another Assembly as they were in critical negotiations with the new government. The Germans meanwhile argued that they promised "never again to be silent in the face of such moments." What to do? Ultimately, amid a close divide, the delay prevailed in deference to our host church. Lastly, I remember the talk by the former LCA Bishop, James Crumley about his attendance in 1947 at the founding assembly of the LWF in Lund, Sweden. As a college student, he was a page and he and other college students asked for an evening with Pastor Martin Neimoeller who had been a leader in the Confessional (i.e., underground) Lutheran movement during Nazi reign. They asked, "when were you most frightened in the war?" He gave the date and the place where he and other prisoners were brought out into the prison yard as allied planes dropped bombs all around them. One of the students said, "please repeat the date and place." He was sheepish in admitting he had been in one of those planes on that very mission. Hence, one Lutheran below as a POW and one as a pilot in the sky above. They awaited Neimoeller's reply, thinking it might be harsh. Instead, he simply said, "Glad you missed." What a story to take home! (Crumley's daughter would be the president of the congregation when we would be called to Ascension, Towson, Maryland, and we would love our visits together over the next few years. Bishop Crumley would preach our installation service in Towson; again, small world connections!)

Our sons made friends in school, achieved awards and recognitions, and played on various sports teams. Parsonage life impacted them with our constant "Guess who's coming to dinner?" quiz. They stayed at the table listening to all kinds of conversations. One son would later write about this in his college admission essay (which he did not share but later was discovered in his room.) He described what it was like to listen to conversations from parishioners to bishops to theologian guests at our table. It was unique. As one would say, "None of our friends have chats like these at their house." The sons' lives certainly were impacted by our parsonage life. Occasionally, as in the college essay, they recognized some advantages; at other times, they resented the parental absences, especially evening visits and meetings and on-call emergencies that would often take us away. The eldest (future nurse) would become President of Virginia Synod Youth Organization, acolyte, "student of the month," honor roll, letter winning athlete, Boys' State Speaker of the House; he would spend four summers in college at NC's "Lutheridge Camp" as a counselor. The youngest, (future attorney) also would win honors as student of the month, honor roll, All Star Little league, city-wide orchestra, acolyte, wrestler and page in both the House of Delegates in Richmond and page in the U.S. Senate. Both seemed to fare well in their "glass house" existence and we are grateful.

When we went to a call committee interview with the Norfolk congregation, it was advent. A large reception room "meet and greet" time was planned. The sanctuary was dark in order to show off the huge Chrismon (decorations meaning "Christ monograms") tree in that room. The next day driving by the church in the daylight with two call committee members, our preschooler son, Stephen, spoke up to say, "I feel sorry for those people there." "Why?" we asked. "Because they don't have enough money to turn on the lights."

The second Sunday I was in Norfolk (1988), an elder patriarch came forward to give me a wristwatch, seeing that I did not wear one and commenting, "This is so you can time your sermons." Ouch. The same person was a "character" all through those years. One Sunday, during the communion liturgy, he noticed some wine spillage. No problem, he came with a mop and bucket to wipe the chancel, while the responses were being sung.

Speaking of sermons, I received an anonymous note from a parishioner criticizing my use of a manuscript since the last pastor used none. I was disturbed by the comparison and took it to the "Mutual Ministry Committee" for discussion. I read it and one member said, "read that second paragraph again." "Oh," she said, "that's Sally so-and-so. She'll send you a letter a month. Ignore it." What a relief when a burden is lifted.

As our sons were older, Judy planned a Christmas Eve dinner at a restaurant between the services to give us some family time together. One time, we had a foreign grad student with us for an Italian dinner and when the spaghetti platters came out, Stephen yelled, "Daddy has the biggest balls." The laughter rolled through the adjacent tables nonplussed by the clerical collar.

Another evening planned at home for Christmas Eve was appetizers and candles after the late service. They waited and waited until food was eaten or put away, candles were extinguished and I can imagine the frigid reception I would have had if anyone had been awake when I arrived. The story went like this: Ushers had departed the church, telling the two remaining pastors that a stranger had passed out on the last pew and they did not know what to do. So, the two of us got him to the front door. Upon hitting the cold night air, he both vomited and urinated and that took some measure of clean-up time. Then we drove him to a local shelter. They had "no rooms in the inn," but said he could stay in the lobby chair. We left. The hour was very late. The next morning after hearing the story, some frigid anger thawed as I called the shelter at 7 AM to check on the man, only to find he had walked out earlier. Fast forward two years and I was crossing the street in front of the church when a man nicely dressed in suit and tie, ran up to say, "Are you the pastor here?" He related how he had been drunk two years before on Christmas Eve and realized we had helped. He said in the intervening time, he enrolled in AA, settled back into a job and life had turned some corners for him. He just wanted to say "Thank you." Good memory.

One couple who wished to get married were civil war reenactors and wanted to have a service in costume with a Lutheran service from that era. They went to Gettysburg Seminary, found a 1860's service they wished to use. I supposed if it did the job 130 years before, it was alright for now as well. The language was very different, but the service was interesting.

One funeral to be remembered was the time the casket was being brought up the front steps. As it began to be rolled down the aisle, a black cat darted from the entrance and jumped up on the casket like a cat's carnival ride was about to begin. Halfway down the aisle, the cat jumped off, headed to the chancel and onto the altar being chased by arm waving ushers while we waited. It was corralled in a side room until later. Is that an omen or what?

Our church made use of chancel dramas for Lenten worship. One couple in a somber, darkly lit sanctuary, portrayed Pontius Pilate and his wife discussing what to do with Jesus. When their dialogue concluded, they went out while thoughtful darkness fit the mood of their departure, when suddenly the microphone picked up his voice, as he said, "Oh damn, I forgot the hand washing thing." The snickers began and the mood was difficult to recover, especially when they joined us for the remainder of the service. Oh well, we try our best! God must surely appreciate our efforts.

One Christmas eve, Judy told me that a couple wished to give a special wine for the celebratory eucharist. OK. When the altar cloths came off the wine goblets, the smell was "different." I asked Judy, "What is this?" "Sherry," she said. I asked, "Is that wine." It was a communion service with more coughs per capita than ever before!

One of our elder parishioners was going to enter the hospital and I got there just as he was checking in. I asked if I might push his wheelchair to his room and they gave permission. I rolled him to the room and he began to move items from suitcase to the closet. The nurse came in, looked at us both and came to me saying, "May I check your bracelet?" I was 48 years old, he was 85 and she came to me! I looked in the mirror to see how bad I looked. I was rather pale. It was Lent. I called him "boomerang Bob," because after I prayed for him, he always prayed for me, the only parishioner who ever returned the prayer!

—The gothic downtown church insisted on using its silver service for coffee hour after church. One Sunday, we all got to the room to find that the whole thing had been stolen. We called the police and they put out the warning. Down the street, two officers had gone in to eat at a fast-food place when a guy entered with a trash bag and clanging sounds in it. Bad move for the thief! An arrest, pictures and soon a return of silver to the rightful owner!

—Sometimes a pastor likes to help t a parishioner in some tangible way. One elder in a rehab place was discharged to her nursing home and once back there, she had a catalogue with something they had recommended she buy. It was a rod across the end of the bed so the covers would not touch her legs. It was just too expensive, she said. I looked at it and thought it was a dowel rod on two pieces of wood with cup holder attachments. I said, I could improvise that easily and cheaply. I went to a hardware store and spent a grand total of $5.89. it worked. However, backing out of the hardware store parking lot, I hit a post that crunched the back bumper and taillight. Cost: $540. I did not tell her; however, the device was not so cheap after all.

Again, one of the stories of this parish's "slightly mentally tilted persons" was a lady in psychiatric treatment. She would call one of the pastors each week and occupy 40–50 minutes of listening time. Sometimes I would lay down the phone and listen while typing and she would stop and ask, "Pastor, are you still there?" "Yes," I answered, and she would continue and so would I. My advice was always the same: "Stay with your doctor and do whatever he tells you." One day she called and said, "Have you seen the newspaper today?" "No, not yet," I said. "Well, they arrested my doctor for killing his wife and wrapping her in a carpet. I told you he was crazy!" I admit, she was better with a change of psychiatrists and meds!

During vacation Bible School two memories come to mind. First, the children's offerings went to purchase a heifer in Africa. When Judy called the organization, she said, "We want it to be a female cow." The voice on the other end said, "You're a city girl, right?" A second time the kids participated in providing a well in Tanzania. The Virginia Synod had a guest clergy from that country attend our week and then the Synod invited any persons to take the trip for the well's dedication in that country. Two of our elders showed interest and were determined to travel. Once there, they decided how to spend their remaining years. They found there were no schools or facilities for children with disabilities. The wife's mother had been a special ed teacher all her life and they decided a new school would be a fitting memorial to her. The couple had three very successful sons and all of them together proceeded to give their money and energies to building this school in Faraja, Tanzania. The school's existence has been a huge success with skills taught and academic accomplishments. These underserved students have found a home with dorms, clinics, classrooms and chapel and the church has embraced this mission. It's a wonderful story (told now in a newly published book).

First Lutheran was the place for one of my most emotional baptisms. The couple had been so welcoming to us with a call committee dinner to discuss whether this call might proceed and during that conversation we found out that both were North Carolinians, had met at the Synod's Lutheridge camp, and the man was the son of the NC Bishop who had ordained me. She was a teacher, raised in the town of my birth (Hickory, NC) and he was a geology professor at ODU. They had a wonderful daughter but subsequently had suffered a miscarriage and the death of twins in a late-term pregnancy. Shortly after we had moved to Norfolk, a new pregnancy was underway. Toward the end of the nine months, I went by the house to offer prayers for the delivery of this baby. The son was born and the baptism was wonderful with many from their NC families in attendance. The poignancy of the event had me thinking about the now-deceased Bishop (their father and now a grandfather) who ordained me and now I was so privileged to baptize this grandson whom he would not see but whose life was touched by my hand with the grace-filled waters of baptism. This was a symbol of what Lutherans mean by "apostolic succession"- the transmission of the faith through the generations. Years later, both son and daughter after college graduations, had us officiate at their weddings. Again, connections beyond coincidences!

Also, the ODU professor of geology was an every-Sunday worshipper and thus a model to our youth. He volunteered to teach the teens with a class so they could see that there was no need for conflict between the creation/evolution debate or between faith and science. (Please remember that I had my worst grades in college in geology. Later, he introduced a geology grad assistant to the church and she was baptized as an adult! Ironies and connections abound!)

Judy enjoyed uncommon success in Christian Education, youth and campus ministries. Because there were some poorer kids in the youth group, each year came to be a fundraising time called, "Youth Scholarship" dinner when the youth would cook, serve and perform an evening's entertainment for the parish. The hall was jammed, and usually $6,000 to $8,000 was given to the youth. Some performances remain emblazoned in peoples' memories. Our eldest performed with his youth group and school classmate, a skit from the "Blues' Brothers." Our youngest performed with a wonderfully flirtatious girl and danced to "Son of a Preacher-Man." Both were show-stoppers! I was a finale act each year, pantomiming some songs, ("Wild Thing," "My Girl," "Born to be Wild," etc.) and the stage night was enjoyed by all.

Global Missions called to see if we could host a visiting pastor from our sister synod in Papua, New Guinea. He stayed in a deployed Naval Officer's home and one day, it was robbed. He was shaken and had to stay with us until the officer returned. I asked him if anything of his was taken. "No," he said, but the previous 6 months he had been given cash gifts of over $3000 to take home. It was under a bed in a briefcase. I got to introduce him to a bank account, but he was not sure if he would get the money back. I took him to a barber shop, but when the hair cut was finished, they spun him around to show him and he asked who that was. He was sure his wife and children would not know him. Everything was new for Matthew. The youth group went to "King's Dominion." He got on a roller coaster with Judy, got off and spent the remainder of the day squatting under a tree, trying to process what had just happened. I took him with me into a car wash. He grabbed the dashboard thinking that a hurricane had come. In a Bible study, speaking of "forgiveness" he said, "I know forgiveness. When my wife walked ahead of me, I was angry and threw a rock and hit her in the head. The Bishop made me ask forgiveness." The cultural exchange was as much a shock to us as to him.

By the mid-90's, Judy was encouraged by many to finish requirements for ordination to enter fully into the Word and Sacrament ministry. With the children now older, she finished course work at Southern Seminary, CPE at Portsmouth Naval Hospital and an internship at Reformation Lutheran in Newport News. The synod candidacy committee recommended ordination and a call was issued from First Lutheran to be Associate Pastor and she was ordained on Sept. 13, 1997. We will always thank the congregation for their encouragement and insistence that she be ordained. A new chapter would begin in her life.

As she ventured into preaching and became a wonderful preacher of relevant stories illuminating texts, no one at First Lutheran will ever forget her "lost sheep" sermon. During the sermon, a man wandered in from the street, walking backwards down the aisle to the front pew. Judy stopped and asked him to be seated while the sermon might continue. He did. But then at the offering, he began crawling on the carpet in front of the pulpit. I handed my hymnal to Judy and said, "You've got the service, I've got him." I went to him and said, "Please stand up and go with me." He said, "I'm crawling like my baby sister." He stood up, looked around at people and said "Martin Luther, 1570." "Close," I said, and out we went. I called mental health and they came to see him. He wore a hospital bracelet and later I found out his meds were off, hence his disorientation. My problem now was with the ushers; after service I chastised them for letting the man enter without a welcome or a bit of screening and I said, 'One of you needed to go out with me in case he had been violent." Their answer was "We thought it was set up as a sermon illustration." OK, it would have been a good one.

—When our eldest was off to college, a lady called to say she had four tickets to an NFL Washington game and would I like them? Of course! Stephen and I would go and I called Christopher to invite a friend from college and we would meet at the stadium for a game. When I went to pick up the tickets, they were not Washington tickets! There were four "raffle" tickets for the real tickets. I hate to disappoint our sons. I got on the phone, tried every way possible to buy four tickets with no success and instead, was able to get Baltimore Raven end zone tickets as a consolation prize! Instead of tickets, instead of "free," I paid a couple of hundred dollars for the "mistake." I never told the elderly woman but c'est la vie!

—These years were spent with much time devoted to extra-congregational ministries. Judy was on various Virginia Synod committees, the ELCA Division for Ministry and representative to the full communion partner church, the Reformed Church in America. I served on the national church council for its "Study of Ministry," various Council committees and, when my term was over, I continued to serve on the ELCA Ecumenical Advisory Committee for six years. In that capacity, I was invited to be on a visitation team representing the Church in London, Canterbury, Geneva, Strasbourg, Istanbul and Rome. I used 5 weeks of sabbatical time for this tour in November to December. A couple of memories:

Our group was invited to Canterbury Cathedral for Sunday worship as guests when the Archbishop would receive the Orthodox Patriarchate for the first time. When we got off the train, with overcoats and scarfs hiding our "clerics," we asked a passerby for directions. After sending us in the right direction, he added, "Today would not be a good time to visit. They'll be having worship." What a cautionary comment for a group of clergy!

We were in the crowds in London waiting to see Queen Elizabeth II enter Winchester Roman Catholic cathedral to also see where the head of the Orthodox church would be welcomed. This would be the first time a reigning English monarch would enter a Roman Catholic church since the Reformation. We had no idea how a vast "protest" crowd surrounded the church, chanting "traitor to the faith," "you're supposed to be 'Defender of the Faith,'" etc. A man asked me who we were and when I said Lutheran, he replied, "Oh, your ordinations are invalid." Such vehemence runs long and is deeply embedded even in "modern" societies.

We were so impressed with Pope John Paul II. He spoke five languages and was very hospitable and warm and kind in the papal apartment where we were received. We were awed by our five days in Rome with his audience and the attention of various Cardinals who had great interest in Lutheran matters.

The next summer was the VA Synod assembly to elect a new bishop for the synod and I was occasionally asked by colleagues if I would permit my name to go forward. I was ambivalent. I could not make up my mind and thus stayed out of conversations without any clear answer. As it happened, I would be fifth in the balloting, but I was disappointed in myself. My speech was not very good. By serving on the national scene, I did not know new pastors in the synod over those last years and there was no reason for me to be known by others. My ambivalence did come through. Leaving parish ministry would be a quandary. It was a weird combo of self-disappointment not to be considered and not to do well "up front."

Attention now turned to a trip the family would take to England to celebrate Christopher's graduation from college. He had interviewed and been accepted to go as a "young adult in global missions" to be in Darlington, England, and just before leaving in June of 1999, I received a call from the Gettysburg Seminary President to come on staff as Associate Dean for Church Vocations and Church Relations. I said, "No." He said, "You're going on vacation. Let's wait and talk about it when you return." We went to England and Christopher and I were a mess. He and I churned over the life decisions and made the trip miserable for Judy and Stephen. Upon returning to the States, Christopher decided to stay stateside with a job as a youth director in River Forest, IL. Then, the call to me came again, this time with some faculty and the person I would work with, calling to plead. Seminary enrollment had dropped precipitously over the years and they wanted someone who enjoyed parish ministry to come and add an authentic voice to "recruitment." What factors went into changing a no to a yes? First, I think the Bishop's election still left me in a disappointment mode; second I believe there was a lingering thought about serving sometime on a seminary faculty or staff; third, they seemed to think that of all the persons they might have called, I somehow had been singled out to do this task. A "yes," would mean leaving Stephen in his senior year in Norfolk and leaving Judy as the interim pastor, allowing him to finish his senior year. Both were consequences of taking a new call. So often, I think of Robert Frost's poem, "The

Road Not Taken" as I was faced with a decision, much like Frost's opening line, "two roads diverged in a yellow wood, And sorry I could not travel both . . ." Hindsight is such a teacher both of regret and wistful wondering. Probably the "No" should have stuck; but a "Yes," changed life once more.

Two weeks before resigning at First Lutheran, I had a tonsillectomy on a Monday, thinking I could be well by Friday. I could not speak above a whisper for two weeks and my last sermon had to be read by Judy. It is a difficult surgery at age 52.

Just before Christopher went off to college, I asked if he would humor me with a special going away party that would be a bit weird. He said, "OK," and I proceeded to gather all the "PK's" in the congregation to come together to tell a funny remembrance of growing up in a clergy family and also to share a poignant story. We had 24 PK's in this congregation! And they did not know each other until that evening. Most PK's were Lutheran, but there was also a Baptist and Methodist in the mix. They included the ODU president, attorneys, a judge; it was quite a group. I began by saying that if anyone needed a therapist by the end of the evening, I was not it but was willing to refer. The age range was 12–80. In summation, the general feeling of parsonage life included these observations: First, they all felt that they lived in a "fishbowl" existence, and everyone knew their business. Second, they all felt pressured to be a leader since others looked that way towards their parents, they should know answers to Bible questions, excel in school, etc. Third, they all complained that their families never had enough money to do what their friends were doing: expensive trips, holidays away, etc. At evening's conclusion our 12-year-old son spoke up. "I have something to say. We got here first to set up and we'll stay here and be the last to clean up." He was correct and no P. K. stayed to help! All-in-all, a remarkable evening.

One of the congregational honors during this pastorate was the selection of First Lutheran in a Lilly grant study that identified what they called the "300 Most Excellent Protestant Congregations in the U.S." in a book by that same name. In retrospect, it would seem that the combination of parishioner energies, outreach ministries to the community and world, and the impact of the church's faith on all ages of members brought about this honor in some identifiable criteria. Sometimes just the right chemistry and conditions happen to produce significant results and we are grateful for the ministry of First Lutheran, Norfolk, VA.

Chapter 15

Associate Dean, Lutheran Theological Seminary, Gettysburg, PA (1999–2006)

This call could have gone either way. I had to learn many new skills quickly. When I arrived at Seminary, I had an apartment on campus, but the central campus building was undergoing renovation. Therefore, our admission office was in student housing and my file cabinet was in a bathtub. Later we would appreciate the move back into spacious, wonderful quarters. By the second week, while sitting in chapel services, the realization came to me that I was really no longer a parish pastor, but a kind of bureaucrat and immediately regretted the decision. It was a dose of regret, my questioning whether it was the wrong decision leaving Judy and Stephen for the next year, all rolled into a depressive moment. The Bishop said he would meet me because I wanted to explore a return from whence I came. Various people calmed me down and Judy, in particular, mandated that a return was impossible. The die was cast. My nephew and his wife had just arrived as he was a first year student and their presence was helpful and stabilizing. The work was before me. My partner in admissions was a wonderful colleague with focus on details and the intricacies of working both academics and synod candidacy concerns together. I was invited to roam the church: congregations, outdoor ministries, our 8 synods and bishops, campus ministries and talk whenever and wherever about parish ministry. Within two years we went from four students under 30 years of age to fourteen. Enrollment increased each of the next six years and it seemed that the seminary was on a better footing. I was invited to preach or make class presentations across the synods including "preaching for the laity," and "church council's organizations, conflicts, etc." and this is where some interesting stories came to be.

I noticed that when I sat in a pew on a Sunday, ushers would often bypass me with the offering plates, noting that I was a guest. I usually had an offering ready and would hand it to the pastor upon exiting. I relayed this to the Bishops who were surprised.

Communion practices varied. I was a guest preacher at one church, where I began at the altar rail and noticed a girl scout, gliding past me, pulling a tray from behind the altar and giving animal crackers to children at the rail (not recommended). Children's sermons were interesting. One used different horses to represent different types of parishioners. I leaned over to a parishioner and said, "I hope the pastor isn't represented by a jackass." By coffee hour, my comment had traveled the room. I learned to be more discreet.

As I supplied one Sunday in a far-away parish, the ushers asked me to please take the cap off a bottle of wine during the consecration so that wine from the bottle could be used by eucharistic ministers later. (I thought to myself, "Jesus can get out of a tomb but can't get into a capped bottle?" But I had learned silence for the sake of discretion!)

One organist did children's sermons. She had exactly 6 treats for the maximum number of children in this small, rural parish. But this Sunday, one had brought a guest. She was neighbors with one of the children and apologized for being one treat short but said she would see him tomorrow with a double treat just for waiting. But a parishioner stood up and volunteered a treat from her purse. As she started down the aisle, the boy shouted . . . "No! I'll take a double on Monday." He knew a good deal. Make him head of the stewardship committee.

My nephew graduated seminary and was serving a parish in York, Pennsylvania. It was the location of an immigration detention center. There he met an incarcerated young man whom he found to be only 16 years old and began to help him acquire English skills and eventually earn his GED. At the same time, our youngest was at the University of Maryland in College Park and was president of the Maryland University College Democrats. He was working for the election of Chris Van Hollen to the U.S. House of Representatives. Nephew Chad wrote me an email that he had no support from any PA politician to sponsor the young immigrant's citizenship application. I was reading his email along with my son's email about a successful congressional campaign; then Chad wrote that he finally had a sponsor: newly elected Congressman Chris Van Hollen! The crossroads of church and state seemed to intersect as the two cousins each had a hand in an outcome, neither knew what was happening! (Connections!)

The Seminary President who brought me on staff came into my office at the end of my first year to announce that his wife's health problems necessitated his resignation and a return to Minnesota. He had promised me a tenure with his presidency but felt I needed to know his change in circumstances. Meanwhile Judy met with the Bishop of our PA synod who said he would recommend her for a Gettysburg parish with two pastors who had served together for thirty-five years and she could then be a bridge interim at their retirement. What we did not know was that they had a reputation for being less than hospitable with each passing female clergy associate (translation: limited ministry and quick exits). It was a less than stellar ideal staff ministry. After three years, she applied for, interviewed and received a call to serve as "ELCA Region 8 coordinator." This meant program staffing for 8 mid-Atlantic synods and their bishops. I referred to her as the "archbishop." This would be one of her happiest calls. However, during these six years she would have multiple back surgeries and it was a hard time for her health-wise. After a podiatrist messed up, she needed a wound vac for a foot infection, so this was a hard time. Through it all, no one would ever know that persistent pain had become her constant companion and continues in her life at present.

I will always remember one particular interview with a prospective student. She was a graduate of a Raleigh, NC college and asked, "Are you Chris' Dad?" "Yes, I am, how do you know him?" "We were camp counselors together at Lutheridge (Arden, NC)." Are you related to Pastor John Cobb (Holy Trinity, Raleigh, NC)?" "Yes, he's my uncle, how do you know him?" "I did some part-time youth ministry in his parish in Raleigh." Then she said, "You're Pastor Cobb for this church vocations interview and I'm supposed to have an afternoon candidacy appointment with Pastor Judy Cobb. Any relation?" "Yes, she's my wife." She said, "Are there anymore?" I said, "Who's your student tour guide? Oh, Chad Rimmer, he's my nephew. Different last name though!" She shook her head! Sometimes, the church world is a small world and, again, connections abound.

Two of Judy's back and neck surgeries were at St. Joseph Hospital in Towson, MD. The son of our parishioners in Norfolk, VA who were integral to the Faraja, Tanzania mission, was the CEO there (another connection). During her hospital stay, we were visited by the local bishop and the assistant to the bishop as I related to them that we might be interested in getting back to a parish call. Judy would later say this too was not fair because she was under sedation and could not speak for herself, but again timing seemed to move in a strange direction. Ascension Lutheran in Towson had two pastors, one retired and one with a new call. Would we meet with their call committee and consider the possibility of a co-senior pastor? What was also intriguing was the fact that this was Judy's home parish where she had gone since second grade (connection). Her parents had moved to Florida and were not there anymore but her Dad had served as long-time treasurer and her mom was the first female Council President. The former bishop was also their former pastor and remained a member for the rest of his life. The call committee interviewed us separately and then together, at which time they told us how different we were. (Duh, yeah.) We accepted this call and moved into a new kind of staff ministry.

CHAPTER 16

Ascension Lutheran Church, Towson, MD (2006–14)

AS AN ORDAINED DAUGHTER of the congregation, Judy had a ready entry into the parish with some elders who remembered her parents. A couple of older folks took credit for having been Judy's Sunday School teachers. We both felt this would be our retirement parish with about eight years until the age factor would clock in. Ascension was similar to First Lutheran in Norfolk, and Trinity in Grand Rapids, MI in that this congregation was also a leading synodical congregation in membership and benevolence giving. This congregation, like others, would present challenges.

On Shrove Tuesday evening, a new couple came to church with two children in tow. The Mom's last name was "Ishida." Arriving on our pancake evening, I surmised they must be Lutheran. I said, "Are you from Japan?" "Yes," she answered. "I am assuming you are Lutheran. Was your Dad a pastor in Tokyo?" I asked. (Now she is looking at me creepily). "I was an intern in Tokyo in 1972 and heard him lecture several times and know that he later served the Lutheran World Federation in Geneva." "Yes," she said, "That's where I grew up." We found she was two-years-old when I was there and now her daughter, introduced that evening, was also two. What a connection of people in our global denomination!

The church had four worship services on Sundays. The attendances did not warrant such multiple times. It seemed to be serving three distinct parishes and one campus/contemporary service on Sunday evenings. The 9:30 a.m. time was a particular stumbling block because it seemed that it was convenient for parents of children to drop them off for Sunday School while parents worshipped, but this also meant that parents were never in study and children were never in worship. While some thought this was an ideal situation, we pastors did not. In all of our congregations we were dedicated to adult learning and in our two previous parishes, the adult Sunday School soon outnumbered the children. We thought this to be a significant goal. Also, this 9:30 crowd was peculiar- almost never participating in the fullness of liturgy, never loosening up to appreciate humor and even guest pastors would say, "what's with the 9:30 folks?" A second reason to drop this time frame was because pastors and musicians could never teach. Adults would seldom return on weeknights for study, so Sunday mornings needed to "carry the freight" of lifelong learning. We had congregational forums on the matter, but it remained controversial until the Council decided to go to two services. We lost about 50 members who would not change their Sunday schedules and who went searching for churches that would accommodate their preferences and convenience. We would now have to attempt to rebuild some attendance.

Around this time, a building renovation program appeared that had been on a "back burner" until the new pastors settled into their routines. The call committee was even unaware that this plan existed. It proposed a $4 million build out and upgrades of HVAC, windows, interior finishes, etc. The fundraising began and secured less than $500,000, so the plan was trimmed to $1.4 million. Property plans have pursued me all through ministry and again, I was forced to go where I did not wish to go.

Once when our two sons came to visit, there was a discussion somehow about Martin Luther and I commented on his dog,

"Tölpel." I said, "in German, it means blockhead." "How do you know this stuff?" they asked. And then they challenged my trivial pursuit about the dog's name. They decided to "google" the question and seek their own answer. When they did, a sermon I had once preached came up with a reference to Luther's dog, "Tölpel." Enough said!

We had such fun with a large number of kids in this parish. With two pastors, one would take children from second grade and under out to chapel after the Gospel reading and bring them back to the sharing of the peace. Here are examples of special remembrances:

After the reading of the prodigal son text, I asked the children "What three gifts did the father give?" They correctly answered, "Sandals, robe and ring." A child raised his hand and said, "But there were two more: a hug and a party." I now ask what five gifts did the father give?

I taught a song to the children about "O Who can make the sun shine? . . . the rain fall . . . the birds sing, etc." and the refrain is "Only God tis true." A little boy said, "Well pastor, that's not exactly how rainfall works, you see a warm front meets a cold front and rain forms." Kids are smart these days.

One child missed the first communion class as we provided children with a taste of bread, wafers and wine. The little boy came to first communion, took the wine and burst into tears, saying, "I thought it would taste like Pepsi."

Two wedding stories:

A couple whose grandmother was a member wanted the wedding of a granddaughter in our church. The parents were prominent Baltimore attorneys, the bride and groom also were attorneys in California. Her name was Suzanne Winters. The church was filled that evening with formally dressed attendees. The bride came down the center aisle, she was blond, slim and gorgeous and I introduced her as Suzanne Sommers (actress)! The congregation regaled with laughter and everyone relaxed.

Ascension has some fine outreach programs: A fifty+ year, well-established preschool (but basically ignoring church/faith;

a long tenured campus pastor who left just before we came; the occasional housing of homeless families over neighborhood objections; a sister parish relationship to the Lutheran Church in Nicaragua; and good support of ELCA benevolence and global missions, a commendable record for any congregation.

Pastor Judy was selected by Gettysburg Seminary for an award in 2011 for "Distinguished Service in Parish Ministry," and I followed with the same award in 2015. We were the first married pastors to each receive the award and we are grateful!

Ascension was the scene of a learning event for me with regard to LGTBQIA issues. In the 1990s with the election of President Clinton, the first Naval officer to "come out" was a newcomer to a Lutheran mission church in Virginia Beach. Our Council President, himself a Naval officer, asked us to write a letter of support for the gay officer and to support the small congregation. Because of so much publicity (the gay officer had been on the "Today" show and the story relayed by national wire services) the parish was embroiled in controversy. Because the mission congregation was receiving this new member, many protested his membership and about 40 members left the congregation which was devastating to the mission and the pastor. The Bishop had backed the pastor and congregational leadership and the division grew. Despite stellar credentials, the officer was forced to resign his commission. As a lifelong Lutheran, he left for law school. Fast forward to a Sunday, when, as seminary staff, I was invited to make a Reformation Sunday presentation to an adult forum at Christ Lutheran Church, Inner Harbor, Baltimore. A man came up and introduced himself. "Pastor Cobb, I have never met you but I wanted to thank you for the letter of support your congregation wrote when I joined the Virginia Beach congregation." Small world again. Now fast forward to a Sunday after Christmas to Ascension, Towson, MD. I saw his name on the visitor register when I had been away post-Christmas. He was now a resident in northern Baltimore and close to Ascension. I googled his name and found a reference to him when he had been a Maryland Synod delegate to an E.L.C.A. assembly considering the gay issue. He had spoken for the issue while the notable opposition comments were made by our retired Bishop who was a member of our congregation! The first Sunday I saw him in the congregation, he was seated across from the former Bishop. Dirk and his partner had an adopted daughter, age 5, and she found a perfect niche with six other girls who all sat in the front of the church, attended Sunday School and choir and all wore pink. She was rooted into the congregation before her parents had made up their minds! In a Sunday School class, they were invited to draw their family units. Another little girl told her mother, "Did you know that some kids have one parent, some have a mommy and a daddy, some have two daddies and some two mommies." Matter of fact and no issue! Dirk became a communion assistant and served the retired bishop. God truly has a sense of humor! (The connections again were obvious: Norfolk, Seminary, Ascension and Christ, Inner Harbor, a congregation I would later serve with a 15-month interim.)

Speaking of the retired Bishop, he was invited, as a long-standing tradition, to preach the Christmas Day sermon. The older he became, the less of a filter he had. Here is the example of the last Christmas Day sermon we asked him to preach. He decided on the theme of "peace." He began with a story of how his uncle had served in World War II in New Guinea and how the uncle had long suffered with "crotch rot." (That left a lingering impression with listeners.) Then, he went to memories of his first Christmas when he realized his parents were Santa, because he had gotten up to "pee" and he saw them putting out gifts under the Christmas tree. (Another lingering impression.) With children listening, two came through the line after worship and one said to Pastor Judy, "Did he say there was no Santa." Judy made a good catch. "No," she said, "He said Santa did not bring the Christmas tree." (Wow—again, no filter).

A young teen from a Gettysburg Seminary family, whose Dad was the CFO, called after college and her marriage to say that the young husband had a brain tumor. Did we know anyone for referral to Johns Hopkins? Yes, one of our members was a brain surgeon and we relayed the name. Later after surgery, the couple had a baby and were back at Hopkins. Knowing that the prognosis was bad, they called to ask if we know a photographer who could take a picture of the threesome since they did not have one. We said "Yes," and our photojournalist called them and they came back to us to say, "I can't believe this. He has the same brain tumor as my brother in NC." She went and happily took the pictures for them. Then later, on a Sunday worship after the young husband had died suddenly, all three were in attendance: the Gettysburg grieving family, the photographer and the surgeon. As I looked out over the congregation, I was not sure they would see each other or know their connections. The surgeon could only predictably attend perhaps one out of eight Sundays but on this day, all were present. During the passing of the peace, I made sure they knew how to connect with each other. (A God moment of connection once again!)

A new bishop was to be elected at the annual assembly of the Delaware-Maryland Synod. Again, I was approached by some but let it drop. I was shocked on the initial ballot to be third in balloting and the top five made rounds to various forums. Three remained at the end, two retired pastors and native of Germany who was synod mission director. He ultimately won with the most emotional personal story and a cheerleading appeal to laity. For anyone who opposed him, he exercised subtlety in slights and retributions whether you had been a candidate or opposed something he supported in debate. I served as a conference Dean and in our meetings, younger pastors would look to me when one of his ideas seemed, shall we say, "irregular." By the end of his term, he had spent much capital on some mission ideas and basically had antagonized various pastors. I met with a neighboring pastor who could be open to a new candidacy at the next assembly if others wished. Judy and I would retire and move away from the synod and had to watch this assembly via the media. This younger pastor was rooted in theology, knew synod staff organizations, was empathetic with pastoral issues and had the confidence of many. We understand as the two went to a fifth ballot, the incumbent asked to make a speech in which he apologized for any slights or failures during his term and pleaded for a second term. The new Bishop was elected on the last ballot by one vote! Without knowing who voted and how, I suspect pastors backed the new candidate and laity stayed with the old. I think it fair to say pastors were joyful and appreciative for new beginnings with equanimity as a modus operandi. Following my votes six years before, I said to a pastoral friend that I was the "Most nominated, never elected bishop candidate in the whole church." (Nominated in VA, NC, DEMD, Lower Susquehanna, Michigan, Metro DC.) I don't think anyone can break that record. God knows what God is doing to nurture and guide the Church! After Virginia, I never wished to hold this office but rather support whoever is in it.

A final funeral story from Ascension. One of the long-tenured members died and while he had married a second wife, there came to be quite a tug between the wife and his two grown daughters by his first marriage. They only agreed on the preference for cremation for the remains. Then a divide occurred over where the cremains would be placed. The daughters would place half of the remains beside their mother in one burial plot and half were given to the second wife. In the ridiculousness of the situation, the wife asked Judy (not me) which half she got!?! Judy replied, "Which half did you want?" She said, "The bottom half, they're going into a memorial bench where I can sit on him." Judy said, "That's what you've got." (Dear God, I hope she's dead by now so there is no chance of her reading this if it's ever in print. But this is the kind of thing pastors have to put up with. Enough said).

Judy's last wedding where I assisted should be mentioned. One of our helpful rehearsal tips was to tell the couple, at the point of exchanging rings, that there seemed to always be confusion over which finger for the ring. Therefore, bring that finger up for the ring placement. Simple, right? At our last Ascension wedding, the actual event, saw the fumbling of fingers. Judy announced over the sound system, "Give him the finger." I started holding back a laugh but then the congregation caught on to what was said, and we shook through the next several parts of the liturgy. It's hard to recover a serious and solemn dignity after it is lost in hilarity! The couple survives to this day with a memory that was only meant to help!

Our time was concluded with the announcement of a retirement party on a Sunday evening in November of 2014. Judy's brother and wife flew in from Seattle; her last living aunt in Baltimore attended and our two sons were present. Bishop Gohl gave a parody of us both that brought both laughter and tears to the congregation, but our minister of music gave a skit that was undeniably the most accurate portrayal of the two of us in a staff meeting that had our sons splitting their sides with laughter. In the balcony were two muppets, Waldorf and Statler, and they had a running commentary of the goings-on. It was a fun- filled time. Gifts were given and we were so surprised with a Viking cruise to Luther Land. We would take one of our favorite vacations ever to celebrate our retirement with our ages 67 and 66, respectively.

CHAPTER 17

Retirement

What's That?

AS WE LOOKED FOR a place to retire somewhere in the mid-Atlantic, Williamsburg came to be that destination. We had hoped to go to Norfolk and rejoin our former congregation, but the pastor seemed hesitant to encourage that decision. So, we looked at other options. We had always invited former pastors back into the life of the congregation and I had twelve good years in Norfolk with my predecessor, and I assumed that is how it would be for us. So, Williamsburg seemed close enough not to possibly be in anyone's way and, at the time, I had my family in NC and our sons in Richmond and Baltimore. In this time, we dedicated some of our life to teaching classes in William and Mary's Lifelong Learning school (I taught *Luther and Reformation* and Judy taught *Louise Penny mysteries*.) Another part of our lives was dedicated to protest marches with the Women's March and the children caged at the border; also the Mueller report and other anti-Trump policies which we deplored.

St. Stephen Lutheran Church, Williamsburg, (my college congregation where we were now members), had one pastor on vacation and another called one Saturday with the onset of flu so could I preach and Judy preside? Sure. That day I preached with various stories again about "connections," but another one occurred that day. Two college students served as assisting ministers that day. They were sisters whom I had baptized at First Lutheran, Norfolk; one of them on that exact day! Connections continue!

Our initial "settlement," in Williamsburg was beginning but then came Bishop's calls. We bought a home and moved in March of 2015. In May came the first call.

The VA Synod Bishop asked me to consider an interim at Trinity, Newport News. That request was in May, with a start date of August. I enjoyed this ministry for 15 months. Bishop Gohl (DEMD Synod) called to bring Judy onto his initial staff after his election and planned to begin with retired pastors who knew the ropes and could help him get started. This too was one of her most enjoyable calls and she thrived in that role. This was to be for only three months. It went for nine. For the last four months of Judy's "tour," I joined her in Baltimore, living in a vacant parsonage in downtown and doing a short interim with a small parish in the city. When those assignments concluded, we went back into retirement mode. We enjoyed coming back to retirement but not for long. The VA Bishop asked if I could go into a Virginia Beach congregation in an emergency mode. I did. Judy was asked if she could steady a small congregation in Gloucester, she did. When those two were wrapped, Bishop Gohl again asked if we could come to the large, metro congregation, Christ, Inner Harbor, Baltimore, whose pastor was retiring, and could we plan to see it through until a new pastor was called? Being close to our son and his life as a Baltimore nurse added incentive to go again. We did. Then, after five months, a lockdown occurred with the pandemic that became a national scourge. We had to give up visitation, in-person worship and learn to create church in a new way. Zoom meetings assembled committees, Council and Bible studies. This church oversaw a preschool, a women's and children's shelter full time; housing for low income seniors with 283 apartments, a parking garage, and a modern campus office building that housed 3 national church ministries (Lutheran Social Services of America, Lutheran World Relief and

Lutheran Immigration and Refugee Service.) Each ministry had governing boards and this was the challenge, especially during a pandemic. In one sermon in February of 2019, I mentioned President Trump by name, in a critical way for his hate-filled remarks. Two parishioners on the way out made it a point to say politics did not belong in the pulpit. Truly, "Jesus talk" can get one in trouble.

Creativity was needed for what lay ahead during pandemic time when the church would be experienced in new ways. For example, we had to buy equipment for live-streaming TV as a skeletal worship crew helped the worship go out over YouTube and Facebook, and had viewers as far away as PA, MI, NC, SC, FL, Ireland and Wales! New horizons were ahead. We served through January 31, 2021, and a new pastor was called beginning February 14.

Upon reconsidering retirement plans, we sold our home in Williamsburg and have returned to a one-floor condo in Norfolk where we can age in place; at the same time the "hesitant pastor" to our reentry retired and the signal is now "please return with a welcome." Also, our sons would come visit us in Williamsburg but then go to Norfolk to visit their buddies. So, we are here with a beloved congregation (and our longest tenure) and many friends.

The stories of biography and church, family, mentors and events leave out so much. The Pastoral Ministry involves thousands of committees, thousands of hours of pastoral visits, conversations, baptisms, confirmations, communions, sermons and funerals (including suicides, accidents, cancer, dementia and every medical illness known to humankind.) Untold in this writing, there are also some seriously deflating moments of parish controversies, contentious confrontations, accusations, serious staffing matters and truly sorrowful regrets. However, pastoral ministry invites a special relational presence that is wondrous in its richness and depth. In every setting of ministry, full time or interim, we have retained and cherished friendships that have endured over the years. We have enjoyed outstanding Church Council Presidents who have admirably served in this important ministry, and we are thankful. We are so enriched and so grateful for far-flung friends who stay with us over the years and across a wide geography.

Judy and I would have a single word summary for it all: BLESSED!

I wish to add two paragraphs about our sons as we are so proud of them both!

Christopher graduated from Maury High School, Norfolk, Virginia and received his B.S. in Communication from James Madison University. He worked as a youth director at Grace Lutheran Church, River Forest, IL, became a paramedic in Greenville, SC, finished his RN, then was employed by "Eagle Med" as a flight transport nurse, became a traveling nurse with a first appointment into the University of Maryland Medical Center, Baltimore, in their shock trauma unit and was offered a full time position remaining there since 2016 in various units including COVID treatment rotations. He has rotated in various departments but seems to enjoy his present position in interventionist radiology.

Stephen graduated from Maury High School, Norfolk, Virginia and received his B.A. in History from the University of Maryland, College Park. He was a page in the VA House of delegates, a page in the U.S. Senate and interned during college for Sen. Ted Kennedy. Working with presidential campaigns, he went on to receive his law degree from William and Mary, served various law firms, was General Counsel for the VA Democratic Party, became Deputy Atty. General in VA and presently is a partner in the D.C. firm of Holland and Knight.

Appended to this writing is a devotional piece I wrote following Christopher's early preschool experience with his quips about church, portions of which were included in the Lutheran Educational magazine entitled *Learning With*. Also, a few vignettes from younger son Stephen are included, and some will duplicate an occasional remembrance in the manuscript, but these true stories are presented here for your enjoyment.

Laughing through the Church with a Three-Year Old

I SUPPOSE WE THINK of him as our "miracle child." The doctors (the best experts on the East Coast) had spent time and tests with us and now were in the office ready to sign papers attesting to such facts so we could move ahead with adoption procedures. But after a few minutes, the red-faced, blushing doctor came back to announce the words, "She's pregnant." I must admit, I secretly like to see the doctors stymied and baffled and science stand in humbled silence before the unexplainable mysteries of God's world. With delight, I related this story of new life to a large adult forum class on Easter Sunday as an example and illustration of the strange workings of God and the gift of hope God gives us at those times when we think the world has had the last word. And so it was that the parsonage life of this pastor and his wife would never quite be the same. I too had been raised as a PK (preacher's kid) and knew of the fishbowl existence and I trembled when I thought of the peculiar role in life that some children are called to play. Anyway, I fondly remember the month of November as his birthday approached. In our church the youth gathered to begin rehearsals for the Christmas pageant and I overheard two children in the following exchange: "We need a real baby for Baby Jesus." "Hey, the pastor's new baby could do it." "No, he can't." "Why not?" "The straw would itch him." "Stupid! What do you think swaddling clothes are for? Besides, it beats a flashlight."

From that conversation, you get the idea that the role of a PK often has the star role in a congregation (center stage) mixed with a human-ness that must be allowable (he itches). Thus is born the perilous role of a PK. The accounts which follow may be recognized as occurrences in the lives of many parsonage families and, indeed, many Christian parents. These vignettes are not fiction. This occurred in the life of our child.

It is a wonder parents continue with children in church. After some traumas and embarrassments, some do, in fact, give up and that's the real tragedy. With our own children, my patient and inventive wife has now lived through some of the difficult episodes. There was the cradled infant in the back pew. The bottle went into the mouth as the sermon began and I knew that the silence would be good only until the last drop. I had my signal (ultimatum?) in the pulpit- soon there would be vocal competition. Later on with a two-year old, a plastic bag filled with cereal with a couple of chocolate chips or raisins scattered in the bag provided a diversion and a puzzle, giving at least a 15 minute quiet treasure hunt (otherwise called behavioral modification or bribery.) One Sunday, our son may have set a record of being taken out of church four times for disturbances. However, (and this is important for parents) he was always returned to the pew because worship was expected and the most important matter at hand.

Having come through some of the battles of parenthood, I remain an advocate of children *in* the worshipping community. The church is impoverished when the young are shunted aside, and it may, in fact, do irreparable damage. Numerous studies indicate the developmental reasons for having children in church. For example, infants simply learn an emotional attachment to what is going on; they discover this event as important to Mommy and Daddy, that we are here together. Next, the children learn to imitate language, gestures, customs and behaviors. Slowly, they absorb the peculiar culture of the Christian Church. Finally, the rest of their lives are spent learning the cognitive or content matters of the faith. Thus, adults in the worshipping community need tolerance towards children and young parents for the occasional disruptions and disturbances. Children particularly need to feel like they are a part of what is going on around them. They can be brought forward to do parts of the liturgy on occasion; they can learn the liturgy by heart and by repeated speaking and singing; they can learn how to make the sign of the cross, kneel, pray, sing and to be silent. Children are introduced to all the new customs and culture of the Christian Church (just as children learn to use fork and spoon and manners at the table.) And of course, the Sunday School and the worship celebrations of the church year calendar will surprise you when seen and heard through the eyes and ears of a child. We are richer for such moments as we shall see . . .

Second Christmas (Luke 2:8–14)

Small children are fascinated with the "things" of their parents' jobs. Soon after he learned to walk, Christopher was exploring chancel and lectern and pulpit, the places where he saw Dad or Mom work. The second Christmas, we wondered how the Christmas story would be perceived. It was a special Christmas too for all the grandparents, the first Christmas when the grandchild could really interact and respond. We had gone to visit my parents. Since my Dad was a pastor too, the three of us walked over to the empty church building on a Saturday afternoon. While we talked in the narthex, I knew Christopher was exploring up front but I didn't know what was coming. I started up the center aisle calling for him when I heard his voice in the chancel. In distinct words he called out a command, "Daddy, sit down." I sat in a pew and looked up front (this was a reversal of roles). I could barely see his head above a pulpit Bible. He said, "My sermon" and then in a clear voice said, "Angels love. Amen." Here was a summary of the Christmas season. My Dad would always think the whole scene was rehearsed (it was not). It was spontaneous. Of all the events and details of Baby Jesus' birth, I still wonder how and why these two words came together in Christopher's "sermon." The angel's love, of course, is a special kind. Angels in the scriptures always seem to preface their purposeful remarks with the words, "Do not be afraid." God's own perfect love casts out fear. No one fears an infant born on that special night. He is God's love, and He is the one casting out fear in our lives. Perhaps an angel's love may be the kind most needed by small children and the rest of us too. The God who is gracious to us insists on coming in the most fragile form of life is a God intent on casting out fear. We do not fear the God of the Christmas manger. He sent us his angel's love.

Ash Wednesday with a Cross in Front (Genesis 18:27)

Our son learned very early to tell whether his parents were dressed to play or work. Civilian clothes meant play and relaxation, while the "work shirt" (otherwise known as a clerical collar) meant the pastor was about to go out for church work. As a three-year old, he knew something was up with a change in a normal day's routine when we wore "work shirts" to the dinner table. This was so infrequent that I knew it would draw his attention and comment. At dinner, I explained that we would be having worship tonight, and I asked Christopher if he knew what day this was. His preschool chapel was given the clue. He said, "I know what day it is. It's trash Wednesday." And me? I had never heard the title quite so mispronounced while being quite so accurate! I knew that I had already been given future sermon titles.

It really is the "trash" in life we talk about when we speak of sin and confession. All of us have so much debris and rubbish in our wake. This day on the calendar initiates a season of reflection on the great struggle of life: sin's condemnation to death—God's gracious invitation to life. Don't ever follow up a child's usage of a new word like "trash" with a request to define it. They walk right over to a trash can, turn it upside down and show you what it means. It is, of course, all the broken, disposable refuse that may very well be the real symbol of humanity. We can throw away our life in pieces or all at once. We can hit the rocks in our relationships. We can die slowly in little regrets or guilty memories. And while we know so well the reality of these circumstances, we also know how the good news is God's invitation to restoration and renewal. God calls us forth as his new creation in each and every day; we can be renewed and made whole. We come alive in his grace. While the world may consider all its efforts to be turning matter into trash, God's main matter and concern is reclamation. God is the restorer and the renewer. God is the One able to transform trash into treasure.

Nails can hurt (Luke 23:32–49)

The story of Jesus's suffering and death are not avoided in Sunday School or church or preschool, just spoken of in a matter-of-fact way. The Biblical accounts were related in story and song through the season of Lent but with none of the usual Christopher commentary. Later, in the spring, we made a visit to our grandparents. They recently had a new roof installed and we were warned that some of the clean-up around gutters still had to be done. Three minutes after arrival, Christopher had gathered a handful of roofing nails and raced over to his family with wide eyes and a quick question: "Did these nails hurt Pop Pop's hands?" "No," we replied. "Well, they hurt Jesus's hands you know." And there it was the commentary on the seasons and lessons just past! For a little child who had experienced little suffering in his young life, beyond occasional splinters and illnesses, it was a good piece of empathy to sense sadness over someone else's pain.

Theologically, we say that Jesus suffered and died for our sakes, and this is true. But also, the one clear lesson of Jesus' own cruel death is his full participation in our life: all of it. "Surely, He has borne our griefs." The Christian's God has never been the detached or aloof deity of philosophy or myth. Christianity is the only faith in which God becomes one of us. The God we know is the God who came down from heaven. The nails hurt. The thorns pained him. The whip cut into his flesh. He bled with pain. Therefore, he is acquainted with our grief, a man who has known sorrow. He often walks into two contemporary caverns of despair- hospitals and funeral parlors. In those places, and others as well, the human body bears the marks of suffering. To those who view the remains, there comes the awareness of life's brevity and its pain. Perhaps it is true that those who stand closest to death know best how to live. But as we live, how comforting to know that the pioneer of our faith has traveled this road. His "having been there," is gospel to you and me. Puncture wounds still hurt and so do nails, and it was a cruel death he died—for us.

Alive (Matthew 28:1–8)

A parent wonders just how the mystery of Easter will be comprehended by the small child, if at all. We adults, if not confused by it all, at least stand in silent awe at the mystery. I knew that on Easter Sunday, Christopher would have heard the Easter words many times (in Sunday School, in a children's video, in a cantata, in sermon and liturgy.) I knew that something about all this excitement would be on his mind; I just did not know what expression it would take or when it would come through his perception mechanisms. That afternoon (after the year's most predictable after church nap), it was Christopher entertaining himself with "peebles" (they were wooden figures for play.) It was with these figures and an old cigar box that the scene was reenacted. One of the peebles walked us to another one at the box and asked, "Where's Jesus?" The other one, throwing the box up in the air, shouted, "You can't find Jesus in the box; he's alive." (All of which is a rather good theological interpretation since it parallels the Gospel accounts; and we were worried that Resurrection was too sophisticated a concept for a three-year old?)

The story and the message must be the church's clearest and simplest: The One who was dead is now alive! No cross, no tomb, no grave, no box can contain him. And with this message is born an imperishable piece of good news, the significance of which is cosmic and everlasting. Wherever death has its hold, God is there as a life-giver. Whether the present circumstance is one of despair or discouragement or death, God will not allow such a power to overcome us. The word of hope and new life will come to us in the most surprising ways as it did on that first Easter morning.

I remember a woman in my office agonizing through a marriage crisis, confessing her thoughts of suicide. She related how she was on the brink of that decision, sitting in a dark room, feeling herself in a dark place. Then, in the light of the kitchen door swinging open, her child yelled to her, "Mommy, we need some popcorn!" The surprise intrusion was a literal lifeline snapping her up out of her grave. This may be a strange way to repeat the Easter witness, but consider the child as an angel standing at the tomb and announcing to the despairing, "He is alive. We are alive." Now go care for someone who needs you. Go get your "popcorn." How great that children can be the angelic agents of assurance. You won't find Jesus in the box. He is alive and so shall we be.

Exalted Body (Luke 24:1–12)

I received a call to another parish. One Sunday morning as we entered the sanctuary for the first time, our attention was drawn to a huge, outlined figure of the triumphant Christ (Christus Rex), raised over the altar and under a sky dome. It was visually dramatic. Christopher was the first to speak: "Hey Daddy, wait a minute, don't they know that Jesus isn't on the cross anymore?" What a summary of our faith! We proclaim that Jesus is not on the cross. Do people know it?

The architectural design of buildings or choice of religious symbols are not the chief clues. Whether people know this will be evidenced in their lives. Those first disciples and their later-day counterparts rush through the world with an excited message to tell: "He is not here, he is risen!" The world's death-grip has been broken once and for all. Christ invites all to celebrate a victory already won. Christ's people have an inheritance of hope with all sorts of practical implications.

This announcement brings to us, as to those first disciples, comfort in the face of mourning. A common experience which comes to all human life is the experience of death. It may begin with a child's love of a pet and an expressed wish to have a funeral for it with all the trappings. Here is an expressed need to say good-bye and a longing to trust all existence to God. Here is a sadness which can never be dodged and a grief which must find expression. It is the Christian faith alone which promises the radical new creation of life in Resurrection. St. Paul proclaims that Christ's own Resurrection is for us like a "first fruit" of the harvest; we get a glimpse and a first sign of all that is to come.

One day the church custodian asked if I could talk to her son about his dog's death. He came in, could barely cross his legs on a big chair and said he was sad about missing his dog; the question, "Would my dog go to heaven?" I told him about a man named Martin Luther who had a dog named "Topel." Luther said the dog died but he would have a golden tail in heaven." The child hopped off the chair saying "I'm glad," and went off to play.

Resurrection is the name of those cumulative experiences which happen to us throughout our years. How many times do any of us count those experiences we call "dead-ends," the "end of the rope," or the "door slammed in our face?" How many times have there been gifts of new beginnings? Christ is the source of these glimpses of new life. He graces us with this wondrous hope. In this sense, we are "born from above," many times over. Christians can testify and bear witness to these truths; that is, any Christian who truly knows that Jesus is not on that cross but is alive forevermore!

Peace (John 20:19–21)

I am sure that all pastors take some local polls at home about various ecclesiastical matters. When a new hymnal was introduced to us Lutherans, I asked at the dinner table what each thought was the best part. Christopher had no hesitation. With an outstretched hand, he said, "Peace to you Daddy, I like that part." What a happy reply to a pastor/father who tended to be most shell-shocked by parishioners' reactions to what for all of us, was a new part of the liturgy. People seemed to have more negative comments on this liturgical change than on any other. Parishioners had called it awkward, contrived, insincere, a bothersome interruption . . ." so much so, that the great temptation was to drop the whole matter and preserve the more formal ritual of greeting and response. But here was a child reaching out with the words and the gesture and saying he liked it best. So, the next Sunday, we let the children come forward at that point in the liturgy and, after a short children's time on the topic, they were commissioned as "passers of the peace." Spreading out into the sanctuary, the small children finally had "peace" with everyone. Looking around, there were no frowns, no scowls, no rigid bodies, no awkward embarrassments. The children had done it again, they had taught us. Through their excited movement and freedom, they invited spontaneous and contagious response to their outstretched hands. Lives are touched with a handshake or an embrace. Christ's own word of "peace," to his people had been spoken; it is a joyous word that speaks both of hospitality and reconciliation. The facades and liturgical coldness melt and dissolve when each worshipper shares the special word and gesture of our Lord. Now I see the whole matter differently. A person doesn't have to inventory his life first and make sure his sincerity is in order; a person doesn't even have to think of his or her own shyness or embarrassment: God help us if we can't greet a stranger in His Name. We are not sharing our emotions or our expressions; rather, in this word and gesture, we pass on the word and action of our Lord to our neighbor. It is not "we" who are doing this, it is Christ: the Risen, Living Lord who has promised to be present where two or three gather in his name. He is incarnate in the word and the touch. He expresses "peace" to all who gather to worship. May we become child-like and carry forth this great commission. Blessed are the peace-speakers and may they become peace-makers too.

Appendix 1

Pentecost (Acts 2:1-4)

As one of the three main festivals of the Christian church, Pentecost, the birthday of the Christian church, was usually given particular emphasis by the congregations we served. Much has been said and done to raise up the theme "Come, Holy Spirit," as prayer, hymns and anthems emphasized the festival. What I did not know was that the Spring emphasis in our son's preschool had been about reciting and memorizing the Pledge of Allegiance. You guessed it: it was Pentecost afternoon, outdoors on a swing set, when I heard Christopher raise up his combination of the two: with an improvised flag atop the swing set, he yelled, "Come Holy Spirit from God, invisible with liberty and justice for all." After a while, you don't stop to wonder how a certain combination of words gets put together in the mind of a three-year old. You simply wait around to wonder what the next heaven-sent utterance will be. Could there be any more accurate description of the work of the Holy Spirit: the invisible power of God at work among his people to bring liberty and justice to us all?

Unleashed in the powerful preaching of the early apostles on that day we call Pentecost, the Church began its great march into the midst of human history. While confronting all peoples with God's salvation in the person and work of Jesus, the Church also noted the significance of this Gospel for all of God's good creation and for the structures and institutions of society. While the expected quick return of Jesus did not occur (which St. Paul especially thought would happen in his lifetime), the Church soon began to consider the coming of Jesus to be out at the end of history: time unknown. The interim (first taken up by the author of Luke) was seen as the place and time for the working of the Holy Spirit. The Gospel would and does today unleash the winds of change in which all creation "groans and strains" in the direction of God's intended purpose. In our age, we see the movements of liberation and the yearnings of oppressed peoples to be free. We see church folks concerned and working in areas of world hunger, disease, poverty, equality, racial justice, invasion of viruses, etc. We see an institutional church groaning to move people into the Gospel imperatives of inclusiveness with regard to age, sex, color and economics. The prayers of the Church in the words of the three-year-old are still: "Come Holy Spirit from God, invisible, with liberty and justice for all. Amen."

Catch the Spirit (Acts 2:3–4)

As a parent, I have no idea where this next episode with Christopher originated. We were traveling over a holiday week and Christopher joined me in the front seat while Judy napped in the back. Knowing he would have to entertain himself, his imagination (and he had plenty) quickly turned him into a "doctor" and a coke straw became a syringe. Using Big Bear as his patient, he announced, "Now hold still, I'm going to give you a shot of the Holy Spirit." (It makes me wonder if he ever heard me say that about some member of the congregation.) How often we wish that God would inject a dose of enthusiasm into the lifeless "dry bones" of some parishioners. I am convinced that if some pastors had some say about their congregation's bodies and behaviors, they would at least insist on these things: First, the bodies would generally lean forward and show a vigorous aliveness. Second, the eyes would sparkle and dance as they do in Christmas Eve merriment while basking in the glow of candlelight. Third, the hands would be in motion to greet friend and stranger and to express peace and hospitality and reconciliation. Fourth, the heads would be attentive to different focal points but especially to word, sacrament, song, prayers and praise. Fifth, mouths would learn to open and shut in response and in song (even monotones.) Sixth, lips would be turned up, if not in happiness, then in gratitude! Such a spirit would definitely be contagious, all for the good.

Lest someone suggest that enthusiasm is the church's panacea, let me note that pastors exercise the greatest caution here. We have discovered that enthusiasm is too often a cosmetic cover-up for shallowness; it is also much too fleeting and temporary. Enthusiasm seems weak and empty when confronted with the deep and often troubling experiences of life. And waving the real caution flag is the experience we have with some persons who seem to only, in a fake way, have cheerleader effervescence, never allowing the heavy and sometimes dark moments to find expression. Rock solid Christians know neither one or the other. We admire the steady ones who simply worship each week, who hear appeals for the needs of the church and respond. They may not get to every church function but may instead be visiting nursing homes. They may pray each day for names in the church directory. They may carry a hot meal across town. They may be supporting a little known project in the wider church. They may be giving a child a scholarship to summer camp or remembering a child's birthday with a card. They may be writing a note of encouragement or support to someone who needs to hear it. Pastors come to know how much of the faith is hidden and unseen. Pastors are in a vantage point to thank God for the unrecognized saints who may lack enthusiasm but never want for their love of the Lord.

Yes, Christopher, I still would like to see more people on fire or get a shot of the Holy Spirit, but we remember what fire can be. It can be giant, leaping, dancing flames; it can be quick, flashy sparks but it can also be slow, steady-glowing embers.

When Jesus Smiles (Mark 10:13–16)

Parents in the church should always be grateful for teachers and others who can excite and love our children while witnessing to the love of God. Our son came home with an excited message one day which I hope he would never forget, "Daddy, I've got good news: Jesus loves little children." The announcement may have been a break-through on two fronts: It got the word across that yes, Jesus does love each and every one of us; and secondly, Jesus does specifically love little children. This latter point may be difficult for the small child to grasp; after all, everything else seems to be for adults and perhaps it too often appears that way in church too. We seldom stop to consider how awesome this big world is for a small child. Consider the church sanctuary. The furniture is too high to climb. Whatever is going on seems to be five miles away down a carpeted highway. The room seems populated with giants, some standing in front of you so you can't see, just like downtown parades. The words have no meaning and sometimes they last a long time. You don't understand what the word "whisper," means and you get a lot of angry looks from parents if you move or ask questions. But there are a lot of colors and music and things happening. You get to put money in bowls and almost always get to color or draw and maybe get a treat. Sometimes pastors ask kids to come up and talk, and on some special days, they may have cookies around church. We had to "unlearn" a bunch of kids who started to use the end of pews like starting blocks so when the benediction ended, they could race to coffee hour. One day, Christopher in the back seat of the car said he would like to be pastor. When I asked why he said, "Because you get to do things, but I am bored where I am." For the child the clothes itch a little, but you're not supposed to pull your shirt out of your pants, and you're never quite sure how to tell your parents that you didn't need to go to the restroom before church but now you do. You're not sure you like the usher who wouldn't give you a bulletin and you wonder why the man in front of you turned around to look at you when you dropped your book on someone's foot. In all of this maze, however, the child is learning some things: church is important to Mom or Dad and a lot of friends come too. Once there, there is some happiness and excitement, and after church children will meet out on the steps to play for a while.

Slowly child, you learn of what is happening in this place, but in the meantime, we adults must remember how it is for you now and perhaps ask how we can make you more of a part in what goes on here. And we must applaud those who excite you with good news that Jesus loves little children.

Expectations (Exodus 16:2–30)

One late afternoon before dinner, the table was being prepared and while Judy and I were busy at the counter, we noticed a little boy peeking around the corner to get a preview of dinner. There, in small glasses at each plate, the dark liquid had been poured and you knew that his wide eyes assumed that a real treat was in store: Coke for dinner! Still, with quiet mischief, the hands went gingerly around the glass, then one big gulp and we turned around to watch. Almost in tears, he complained, "It's not Coke . . .aughhhhh!" From that moment on, it didn't matter how much we talked about nutrition or waiting to drink with the meal, there was no convincing Christopher that prune juice had any benefit whatsoever! He expected one thing, got another and was bitterly disappointed.

How often do our expectations deter us from the full participation and enjoyment of the moment? Looking back into the history of God's people, this has been a recurring problem. An apple that wasn't all that great after it was tasted; God's promise of deliverance for the people of Israel, which was met with groaning and grumbling and complaining when the journey became hard and the rewards few; even Jesus disappointed many of the people around him who expected someone or something entirely different. Some looked for a political leader and worldly kingdom builder; some looked for the miracle which would avert the trial and cross and crucifixion. Many people were bitterly disappointed when their expectations never came to be realized. But this hints at the real problem, doesn't it? Our expectations and God's may just be two different things. When you are ready to gulp a sweet, syrupy cola and instead, your mouth puckers from the taste of a bitter, fruity roughage, you may not be very excited about the drink no matter how good it is for you. So, what are your expectations in life? A desire for smooth and easy living, stability, health and happiness, calm and non-threatening environments and experiences? What if God puts us into the midst of something else? What if we're going into the valley of the shadow of death or are bothered by some kind of trouble we did not ever expect? What if we are confused or uncertain? What if life seems stirred up and chaotic? Can God be the leading hand in these places too? The witness of the scriptures is a resounding YES! God may be the still, small voice in the midst of the whirlwind. While our own expectations about how and where our life will be ordered may give us a certain expectation, God may have something different in mind. It takes a risk of faith to turn loose what we expect in order to be open to what God is offering. And to those with eyes to see, and ears to hear, his gift will always be one *for our sakes.* Always. So that we might have life and have it abundantly.

Get the Message (I Thess. 1:2–8; I Peter 1:23–25)

On one of those days of rushing around, I had Judy and Christopher with me in the car and made a quick stop at the mailbox to grab the mail. Dashing back into the driver's seat, I quickly did a sorting job on the dashboard. There was my mail, Judy's mail and the church's. I noticed Christopher's mood begin to change about the same time as the lower lip began to quiver. "I get mail too?" He asked with sadness and hope at the same time. I made a quick re-run through my mail and knew one envelope was a mass mailing from an institutional church furnishing business. "Here, one for Christopher Cobb," I said. He spotted a cross on the envelope and as quickly as pouts turned to smiles, he said, "Look Mommy, it's for me and it's from Jesus. Read it."

She opened the letter and began: "Dear Christopher, I love you very much and signed Jesus." Is the reading a deception? I think not. Everything about the Gospel tells us how God has persistently sought the means to say just this word to his people. God's one message has had the same, consistent theme since Genesis. For God so loved the world that God created. God so loved the world that God gave the law. God so loved the world that God sent the prophets. God so loved the world that in the fullness of time God sent his son, as our Lord and Savior. God so loves us that the Word is among us again in Word and Sacrament. Also, God has personalized the message just as much as an addressed envelope: the person is touched as another says, "I baptize YOU . . ." each of us is specially addressed as the words of the communion tell us, "Given and shed FOR YOU." God keeps coming; we need to hear and see. Sometimes we reject the message thinking such a Word could not possibly be meant for us. Sometimes, we are suspicious, thinking that such grace must have some "postage due" on our part. Surely, we must earn or pay for this invitation somehow. Sometimes, we lay it all aside, put the message unopened on a shelf, put off by its plain wrappings in common people and in such ordinary elements like water and bread and wine. One thing though: to God the addressee is never, "unknown." Our creator God knows precisely to whom his love is directed; it is to each unique and special person created and loved by God. Yes, Christopher, the message is from Jesus; his love is addressed to you.

When Life Gets Gritty (Job 30:26–27)

The ministry is not the kind of vocation that you can ever compartmentalize or leave behind you on vacation. The Jesus of the church is also the Jesus of vacations too. And, as any Christian child builds his or her personality structures and various components of cognitive content, Jesus is related to whatever he or she happens to be doing at the moment. In another city, among unknown children, the church-child may teach the whole group the words of the liturgy or some memorized hymn. One may invite the neighbor to attend their church or Sunday School. It is all so natural and matter-of-fact for children and we adults must learn from such naturalness and lack of inhibition.

On one of our restful beach vacations, far away from work shirts and crazy schedules, all was going well until an angry, pouting Christopher, holding his swimming trunks, came in my direction to angrily demand an answer to the question, "Why did Jesus make sand?" At that moment, it seemed that all of that sand was inside his swimming trunks, so why would Jesus create something that could irritate us so? Somehow, I'm sure, Christopher's question is related to the same type of question asked by Job thousands of years ago. It is the question of suffering and irritation and of the haunting, "Why?" To every parent, there comes the moment of feeling totally inadequate in the face of such inquiries. That day, I am sure I side-stepped the question and went on to respond to crises by mumbling something about how Jesus made the beautiful beaches, sand and water, and how we must take care to avoid the trouble that we can invite upon ourselves. And Jesus of course, gives us families and friends to help us react to the trouble (off come the trunks, the towel brushes the bottom, and the trunks are pulled back up.)

I am sure that no theologian has ever given adequate response to the question of suffering. What we have, however, is the community of the Church to help us in the face of any disaster. Look at what God has set in motion to respond to the gritty irritations and troubles in this world: the affluent are called to feed the hungry; the sick are cared for; the elderly are housed and loved; and thousands of volunteers in community organizations offer time and talents to children of all sorts and conditions. The "sand" we may never understand. The help is heaven-sent and close at hand.

Peace, Be Still (Mark 4:35–41)

The preschool had just read the account of Jesus stilling the storm. The eager faces listened with awe and wonder at the power necessary to accomplish such a feat. Next, the teacher wanted the class to role play the episode. We outlined a boat with masking tape and some were disciples in the boat; some were noise makers like thunder and wind and rain; someone flashed the lights like lightning. So, why does the PK always get to play Jesus? Anyway, on that day, we had dressed our son in popular "underoos" (superhero underwear), a mistake beneath his outfit. As Jesus, Christopher stood in the boat and at the appropriate time ripped open his shirt and shouted, "Shazam, shut up." Only an underoo "Shazam" shirt and a superhero could have such power. The teacher was speechless with the improvised interpretation!

To this child, the power of Jesus described in the story represented "superpowers." It must have been so with the disciples as well. So impressed were they that this friend of theirs became a kind of stranger in their midst. They whispered in frightened wonder, "Who is this that even the winds and the sea obey him?"

Our children grasp who He is. He is the Lord of power and might. While he is a superhero and super friend, he is also known as the humble servant of love and grace. After all, in this one stroke of a commanding word, hadn't he taken away the disciples' fear of death? Doesn't he still do this for us? There is no life-threatening episode where the words of Christ—Peace or Shazam, Be Still—cannot be heard as the Lord's word of power and grace. Thank God for such super comfort!

Jesus, Sick? (Romans 12:15)

I am sure every parsonage family has experienced a child's jealousy toward the church which seems to take a parent away from them,

especially due to unpredictable schedules. One of my earliest memories is standing in the driveway crying as my Dad's car left on another emergency and I couldn't go with him. One day our own PK knew that something was about to happen. The phone rang and I dashed upstairs returning with my "work shirt" on. Christopher's interesting comment to all of this brought the words he had overheard about hospitals and the sick together with the Jesus symbol always carried by the "work shirt." And so, with a jealous and subtle understatement he asked, "Does Daddy have to go out? Is Jesus sick again?" Think about this for a moment as I did on the way to the hospital. All of these were put together in the mind of a three-year-old: Jesus, prayers, hospitals, sickness, and Daddy the church person (parson). And they do go together. The Spirit of Christ which we carry in our being must come in these times of illness, disease and accident. Prayers offered in the name of Jesus ask for guidance, patience, understanding, healing and comfort. The representative of the faith community is called to go in the name of Jesus, carrying the expressions of care and hope gathered up and offered by all the faithful. Jesus is present in the communication of the caring. The three-year-old child may miss the mark slightly with his composite imagery, but not by much. Jesus is sick in the body of the ill, but children also see that the same Jesus is the healer and comforter. And some are asked to put on the "work shirt" and go in the good, strong name of Jesus to share our needs and hopes in prayer.

Obedience (Gen. 3:1–24)

Some Sundays you can get a comment from your child about what they learned in class, and sometimes not. In those times when you hear a summary of some lessons, don't be surprised if it's a little bit fractured or skewed. One Sunday lunch, we heard the replay about two people named Adam and Eve. According to the gospel of St. Christopher, "Adam and Eve were two good people. God told them, "don't eat the rotten apples." They ate the rotten apples, threw up and died." I love the fractured story (teachers: don't despair; it's not your fault, children have a mind sieve to sort it out in new versions.) I suppose there is an early theological formulation going on here in the three-year-old's world. The consequence of our disobedience will be disastrous. The Garden of Eden is the story of disobedience and rebellion. Humankind has been in trouble whenever and however the hearing and doing of God's word has gone unheeded. It seems that we are born to test the limits and parameters of our freedom. The toddler must have the other child's toy. The glass must be thrown or dropped. The bowl must be turned upside down. The crib must be climbed over. The door must be slammed even before learning the fingers must first come out of the door frame. Parents become hoarse with shouted words like "stop," "don't," "no," or "wait." Parents soon think of themselves as lawgivers, soon become tyrants. The ensuing guilt over "nay saying," soon becomes its own kind of burden. Parents do learn that rules and discipline have a purpose. The motivation is always love for the child. It's the parents' prior knowledge of neglect for the laws and rules and parameters that can literally mean disaster to life and limb. Parents need to know that law is not the end in itself, love is. It is the happiness and well-being of the child that are uppermost in the teaching of rules and disciplines. We are a disobedient and rebellious people, and our actions can have terrible consequences; thus, the law of God. Such laws are not for the sake of cruel punishment, but for the sake of our very lives. God, who is God, would do no less.

The Good Ending (Psalm 119:105)

It is a delight to watch a child at age three or four become a "parent" to another child. When little Beth, one and half years old, walked into our house, Christopher took her over with hugs and kisses and with a high voice reassured her that he would take care of her. He said he had a story to read to her when she sat down (he helped her down with a thud.) From the bookshelf, he pulled the "Children's Living Bible," and explained, "Beth, there are a lot of bad guys but don't worry, the story turns out all right." I couldn't have said it better myself. The story calls to mind two hopes: first, hope that the scriptures as the chief book the church ought to readily be available and in use around the home. There is a naturalness with which the stories of the Bible can be taught at home (and with some of them, we suggest that "parental discretion is advised," had you ever considered that the Bible moves between PG and R ratings?) Second, we must hope that the story ending is known by the child: that each episode ends with a certainty that God is faithful and remembers God's people and saves them from trouble. If no other concept is learned, this one will prove to be a great assurance all through one's life. The Christian faith has the character of a story, a narrative. There is content to this unique and peculiar story and its chief character and plot set this story over and above every other story that we know. It is His-story and ours. We are the rebellious, the angry, the confused, the stiff-necked and hard-headed, the depressed, the discouraged, and the sick. Also, we are occasionally the devoted, the faithful, the joyous, and the committed. God deals with all of us in His-story. And part of the interpretation and translation occurs when the Biblical story comes to be seen as our story. The sooner a child, or any of us, enters the story, the sooner we are immersed in the world's greatest reality: God's love for us in Jesus Christ.

A Sacrament: The Bath (Matt. 28:19–20)

In our parishes, we have the frequent custom of inviting a group of children to come forward at the point of baptism when this special liturgy is celebrated in the worshipping community. Children stand in wide-eyed wonder when the baby is essentially "graced" in this precious Sacrament. Some parishes may miss a great opportunity for teaching and for informal sharing if a group of children is not invited to gather around the font and watch what happens. We generally do all the readings up to the point of the baptism and then invite children to gather and watch. In conversation about what is happening, most will readily grasp the connection with a bath. We can speak of "washing away sin," or, we can speak of water as a nurturing agent of growth or of water quenching thirst in the sense of its use in the Gospel of John.

While our sons have stood in awe of these events and always make some mention of "baptism" (they do know this big word and what it means), they have never gone very far in questioning what is being done. Once, after a baptism, Christopher brought me his favorite stuffed animal, "Big Bear," with the proposition: "Daddy, baptize him."

(Suddenly you wonder if the theologians will take away your ordination papers if the word gets out.) You say something like, "Christopher, since the toy is a pretend animal why don't you have a pretend baptism?" You ask him, "What would you say?" And he gets it: "I baptized you in the name of the Father and the Son and the Holy Spirit. Daddy, I forgot the water." "Pretend" (the stuffed toy is to be dry washed).

What a great intuition the child has about this Sacrament of the Church. He has understood that the first and main impulse of the Christian is to bring the most precious and treasured lives we know to the God of grace, the God to whom we offer up the ones we love. Many reasons bring us to such a decision. We have the command of Christ to baptize, and among God's faithful people there is the impulse to publicly affirm the gift and grace of new birth. While the first birth usually occurs in the antiseptic environment of hospitals, the second and most important new birth occurs in the midst of a joyous, celebrating, worshipping community gathered in Jesus' name. Here he accepts our precious lives offered up to him; here he marks us with the sign of the cross and promises an eternity of his love. Such a hope for a baby or even a pretend toy is the greatest gift possibly bestowed on the ones we love.

A Sacrament: The Meal (I Cor. 11:23–26)

When Christopher was two years and three months old, the night was Ash Wednesday. Infants and very young children were brought to the communion table for a blessing. Judy had rehearsed church etiquette with Christopher for some time, especially at the altar rail where everyone knelt. She made some trial runs in an empty church to stress the how's and what's. That evening after I had commandeered Judy and blessed Christopher, and moved along the rail, he boldly stood up and announced, "Daddy, I'll have some Jesus bread too."

Two other episodes are remembered. Some weeks later at the evening meal, the menu was pancakes. After the table prayer, he took a piece of the pancake, turned to me and said, "Daddy: body of Christ for you." The next episode came later one day in my study. I had a private communion set on the desk and I took a phone call. Christopher, looking at one of Daddy's "work cases," went to the communion set, poured a pretend liquid into one of the small glasses, turned to Judy and said, "Take this; this is the most wonderful wine of your life." Through all of these things in the span of a year, some significant learning has occurred. Jesus' bread and the wonderful wine of life gives us a rather accurate summary of the Church's unique meal. For the rest of his natural life, Christopher may add layers of cognitive content and understanding of what this meal is about. Our church caught on to how children via their baptism can also be admitted to the church's meal. The meal has no admission ticket according to our age or understanding. When St. Paul wrote about the meal, he was discussing what "discernment" meant in terms of setting it against the frivolity and divisive class status that was being practiced by the Corinthian church. The church looks to a parental guide where parents are regular in attendance and at home model the naturalness of talking and speaking about matters of faith whether in our "rising up or sitting down" (Deuteronomy 6: 4–9), whether in our work or in our leisure. Children can grasp the bread and wine, the presence of Jesus, the table where Christians gather to receive the good gifts of God. Let it be so. The most "wonderful wine of our lives" is too good to miss.

Stephen, our second child, had some moments too (but they might necessitate another writing.) Here are a couple of examples:

Youngest child ran up to me after church, wanting to know where are the ducks? For the life of me I could not unpack what he meant. Once we were in a longer conversation, he said something about singing with the ducks. Finally, I understood. I had announced the singing of the doxology. I understood his translation!

The new speaker system for the church was installed with speakers under each pew. At about age 1 1/2 he heard me making announcements and the voice under the pew was being heard; he dove to the floor saying, "Daddy, Daddy." Obviously, the voice was in search of a body.

The associate pastor talked with children about what a difference the water makes in baptism. He held up banana chips and a real banana and asked what was the difference. He gave each child a banana chip as they returned to the pew. Pastor went to the pulpit to begin his sermon. Stephen went back to the pew, tried the chip, said yuck, and headed back for the real banana. I thought he was coming to sit with me at the lectern. I put out my arms to receive him. Nope, he grabbed the real banana and headed back to the pew. The congregation went into laughter. The pulpit preacher heard laughter but did not see what has happened. He had to regroup and go again.

Just after he could read the bulletin and order of liturgy, he told me he was disappointed this particular Sunday, because he said, "they listed a passing of the peach." Watch out for the secretary's typed mistakes. Children are watching and sometimes reading.

What, Then, Shall We Say about Children and Church?

Too many folks think of the church's worship as an adult activity. How paternalistic we are, to pat our children on the head while standing over them with our maturity and knowledge and cognitive content. These thoughts coupled with the "noise" of children and the accompanying embarrassment of parents have provided the impetus to populate church nurseries or worse yet, "junior" or "children's church." My underlying bias first, as a childless couple and later as pastor/parents has been this: worship is the gathering of all the baptized people of God. All of us should recognize the obvious:

Children will squirm and cause distraction. Etiquette and disciplines of behavior must occur in church just as it is done in the home and school. Some things are expected and some things are not permitted.

At times, noise must be acknowledged and dealt with; a parent may have to remove a child for a time to a narthex or side room and return. A nursery may occasionally be used when the child arrives at a particularly difficult stage (16–23 months seem to be a common, difficult time.)

The church should practice surrogate parenting and especially grandparenting. What a gift someone could offer a harried parent with a request for the privilege of letting a child sit with someone special during church or special occasions. Predictably better behavior will occur; parents get a break and a child gets a new friend. Parents of course, won't ask; willing worshippers must simply take the initiative.

In the introduction to these vignettes, I posed the rationale and direction as to why children must be an inclusive part of the worshipping community. To summarize again:

The Christian Church is a "culture," with its unique language, gestures, signs, symbols, songs, creeds, actions, prayers and liturgies to be learned.

Learning occurs emotionally. With the infant, the emotional attachment to parents is obvious. There still will be early learning that church is important to Mom and Dad; each week, there is singing, crowds of people, bright colors, etc. The infant soon knows that this event has importance in the routines of parents and there is even an imprint about Sundays in the week's rituals.

Learning occurs through imitation. By age two and three, children can imitate behavior: those associated with church may include kneeling, praying, sign of the cross, movement, singing, memorization of a creed, Lord's Prayer, liturgical chants and responses. Church etiquette and behavioral expectations can be learned.

Learning will occur cognitively. The child will use their brain to learn factual content; information comes in and is assimilated. Today, we think our church experience is purely intellectual. The best sacramental and liturgical theology has always suggested that God has chosen all of our sensory channels to pour forth the Gospel. Too often we think of the ear and the head connection with the Christian faith. Learning channels include these but it can also be found in our seeing, tasting, touching, and smelling.

There are numerous reasons to argue for the inclusive nature of the church. Jesus said it best: "Let the children come to me and do not prevent them; for such is the kingdom of God." What joy and spontaneity and wide-eyed wonder they bring to the gathering of all the people of God! Welcome them.

Bibliography

Buechner, Frederick. *Listening to Your Life: Daily Meditations with Frederick Buechner*. Compiled by George Connor. San Francisco: HarperSanFrancisco, 1992.

———. *Now and Then*. San Francisco: Harper & Row, 1983.

Kolden, Marc, and Todd Nichol. *Called and Ordained: Lutheran Perspectives on the Office of the Ministry*. Philadelphia: Fortress, 1990.

Luther, Martin. *Letters of Spiritual Counsel*. Edited and translated by Theodore G. Tappert. The Library of Christian Classics 18. Philadelphia: Westminster, 1955.